STARTING YOUR BACKYARD HOMESTEAD 2-IN-1 SURVIVAL COLLECTION

STARTING YOUR BACKYARD HOMESTEAD + SURVIVAL HANDBOOK OF MEDICINE - THE #1 BEGINNER'S COLLECTION FOR STARTING YOUR BACKYARD HOMESTEAD

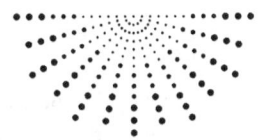

J. B. MAXWELL

For my exquisitely beautiful Wife,
Who has always been my warm sun.

TABLE OF CONTENTS

STARTING YOUR BACKYARD HOMESTEAD

STARTING
— YOUR —
BACKYARD
HOMESTEAD

MY FAVORITE GARDENING TECHNIQUES, PERMACULTURE
DESIGNS, AND PRESERVING PROCESSES FOR BEGINNERS

J. B. MAXWELL

INTRODUCTION

A society grows great when old men plant trees whose shade they know they shall never sit in. – *Greek proverb*

The crisp Pennsylvanian air that fills my lungs every morning as I step outside my house is a feeling I don't think I could live without. I wake up each morning to the sounds of my homestead all around me, my son's feet pattering away on our hardwood floors, and my wife reading and sipping her coffee. This peace and oneness with nature is central to my family, and creating this balance has been central to my own development. Growing healthy, clean, and organic food with the help of my family has created a beautiful cohesion of self-reliance and a reduction in harm to the environment, and to my wallet.

A couple of days ago, my ten-month-old son took a bite of a fresh vegetable from my garden. At first, he made that shocked face that babies make when they are trying something new. Then, with his four little teeth, he took a bigger bite followed by an "Mmmm" while taking more bites and dancing in his high chair. He was excited, and his excitement felt electrifying to my wife and me. I was reminded that providing healthy and delicious food for my family was one of the main reasons that I started homesteading.

I started homesteading eight years ago and I haven't been able to stop since, nor do I plan to. I have had two properties that I have created homesteads on. One was a little less than a full acre and the other was a full acre. Having the space and flexibility to test what type of farm I wanted to cultivate made the process of discovering my love for nature, and the reliance I wanted to have on it, crystal clear. The hard work that I put into developing my homesteads ultimately means that when I enjoy the farm's foods with my family, they are that much more delicious. There is something about taking a bite of one of your own fresh vegetables that makes the taste unrivaled to anything you could buy at a big-box grocery store. Taking control of my food and having a hands-on mentality to provide for my family has created innumerable benefits to my life.

Please don't misunderstand me. I can't say that it was always smooth sailing. There were a lot of moments where I felt alone, confused, and silly for working on farming projects. I was motivated to try to find strategies for homesteading on my own and had many embarrassing setbacks along the way. Since then, I have dedicated my time to researching the best strategies for your first homestead so that you can avoid the silly mistakes that I made. I have always had a passion for helping others and providing advice where I can. When I found out about this style of farming and pursued my passion for self-sustaining home gardens, I realized that the intersection between helping others and practicing homesteading was the perfect place for me.

Since my first trial-and-error period, I have dedicated my time to researching, practicing, and implementing different homesteading principles in order to amass blueprints that anyone can use. There are many steps that go into beginning your farm and there are many types of homesteads from which to choose. Whether you are a college student looking to live in a tiny home and plant your own sustainable garden or you are a family of five looking to go off-the-grid on a large plot of land, these blueprints will help you begin your journey.

I spent so many hours with a bruised ego and damaged pride after making many mistakes on my first homestead, but now the confidence that I have as a result of getting it right is unparalleled. I hope to show you all the ways that homesteading can work for you. Not only will this guide be a helpful resource in your journey, but it will also serve as a time saver. If I had someone to lean on when I was beginning, I could have streamlined so many of the systems I was attempting to create. Now, you will have this guide to lean on when you are beginning your exploration into homesteading.

The benefits of cultivating your own land cannot be overstated. Nothing is better than growing your own crops, giving them to a loved one, and watching their face light up as they take their first bite. Homesteading is the practice of finding a balance between yourself and nature, and is also a way to bring together a community. You have so many options when you begin, and there is potential for true reformation and recalibration of yourself. While I won't claim that this is a book on how to find a happier version of yourself, I believe that beginning a farm can greatly assist in that process. No matter what kind of journey you are on, homesteading can be there to help.

1

THE HOMESTEAD MINDSET

*B*eginning your own homestead is a daunting process. There is no doubt in my mind that you may have a thousand different ideas for how to approach homesteading, but finding the perfect starting place is a challenge. The best place to begin is to understand the homesteader's mindset and what it will require from you is pivotal to beginning your journey into homesteading. There are six mantras that are essential for farmers to keep in mind:

- Think long term
- Raise the odds for success
- Focus on work they love without getting distracted
- Manage their lands and themselves
- Rest after they have given their all to the day
- Are grateful for the outcomes they get (Animated Spirit, 2018)

While all of these mindset prescriptions may seem very stringent, there are a lot of benefits that homesteaders can get from them. When you are starting the planning process for your homestead, it is important to plan for the entire year. The first mindset that a homesteader needs is that farmers think long term. During the planning process, plan for the entire calendar year. Having the ability to plan and think long term will allow you to keep in mind some smaller goals that you'll need to achieve during the year to sustain the homestead. I suggest getting your hands on *The Old Farmer's Almanac* that is published each year, or visiting their website. In each edition, the Almanac publishes seasonal forecasts, tips about gardening and farming for long-term success, and the way that astrological changes can affect your farm. Planning for your specific year and the region of the world that you are in will be central to maintaining a homestead year-round. The first mindset that needs to be cemented is the ability to plan long term so that you can raise the odds for your success.

This brings me to the second mindset shift that needs to occur: farmers raise the odds for their success. Success on a homestead can look like a lot of different things depending upon how you choose to structure your homestead and what your eventual goals are. The general principle is to figure out, based on your own goals, what obstacles might impede the success of your homestead. Remaining in tune with permaculture patterns, weather patterns, and any ecological events that are happening in your region of the world will be essential to your success. It is always better to fix problems or adjust for any obstacles you come across when you see them and not put them off. Putting off obstacles will increase the likelihood that those obstacles become bigger and more difficult to manage. I will address more exact ways to plan for obstacles when I discuss hardiness and perma-culture zones, but for now, the mindset of raising the odds for success is being sure that you hold yourself accountable for fixing problems right when they come along and preparing for obstacles early.

Remaining on task and addressing issues on your homestead when they come up goes hand-in-hand with the next mindset that is neces-sary for every homesteader: farmers focus on work they love without becoming distracted. There are so many moving parts to a lively homestead that you are bound to become distracted or taken away from tasks you are performing. Commit yourself to a task and avoid heading down another path. Completing tasks on your homestead will be central to the growth and development of your homestead. If you are someone who struggles with becoming distracted, find an accountability partner. Plan, raise your odds for success, and be consistent with getting through tasks that will make your homestead thrive.

Many people begin their homesteading journey with families in tow. Beginning your homestead with your family is a great way to find a balance for the next mindset shift that needs to happen: farmers manage their lands and themselves. Having people in your immediate community, like your family, will aid in your journey to solidifying all of the homesteader's mindsets that are essential to success. When you are beginning a homestead, finding a balance between how much you work and managing yourself will also lead to long-term success. If you get burnt out too quickly from trying to tackle too many tasks, not sleeping enough, and turn homesteading into a chore and not something you love, you will inevitably abandon the project. Family can help you find this balance of managing yourself while you manage your land. Having people to hold you accountable and people who are relying on you will encourage a sense of self-actualization. You are the one who is caring for the well-being of the people around you, your-self included.

Resting when you need to will also help you to manage yourself and your land. Farmers rest after they have given their all to the day. This part of the homesteader's mindset is the equivalent to self-care. Do what you love on your farm, remain consistent in finishing tasks, and rest when you are finished. Having a balance of work, time with people you care about, and rest, will help you find an internal balance to ensure that your homestead persists for a long time.

The last, and in my opinion, the most essential, mindset to have when you begin homesteading is that farmers are grateful for the outcomes they attain. There will be times when all of your goals for your homestead are coming to fruition and there will be times when that isn't the case. Both outcomes are perfectly acceptable. No matter what outcome you get, you will learn and grow for the next time. Be patient when things don't go according to plan and reflect on how you are able to develop better systems and management for next season.

BEGINNER'S MINDSET

The homesteader's mindset is definitely the aim of developing a homesteading system that will work for you, and a great way to build that is the beginner's mindset. One study done by Harvard Business School professors Amabile and Kramer outlines the benefits of adopting a beginner's mindset and overcoming the obstacles that you may face. In the study, the researchers were specifically looking at workplace management, and for you, your home is your workplace (Amabile & Kramer, 2016).

Establishing the beginner's mindset starts with the progress principle. The progress principle is the notion that the best way to maintain a healthy balance of work and productivity is to see meaningful progress being made and to celebrate that progress (Amabile & Kramer, 2016). No matter the scope or amount of the progress you are making with your homestead, all progress is pushing you toward more productivity. The study also lays out different types of work-time triggers that can occur to either boost or diminish our feelings of accomplishment. *Catalysts* and *nourishers* are events that support and encourage our work. These events are essential to instilling a beginner's mindset. For example, if you are planning your homestead and you show your designs to a family or friend and receive praise and constructive feedback, there is a catalyst present to support your work and you will be nourished and encouraged to continue. There are also *inhibitors* and *toxins*. Interactions that fail to support you or discourage progress can lead to diminishing returns on your efforts. If you show your design plans to a family or friend and they only critique, question, and admonish your work, there is very little encouragement to continue working. In order to reap the most benefits in the beginning phases of homesteading, encourage yourself to continue working, support yourself through self-care and rest, and be patient with yourself if you make mistakes. If you have other people around you or who will be living on the homestead, ensure that those people are catalysts and nourishers who can support your progress. Associating positive emotions with the progress that you'd like to make will spark a chain reaction that will encourage you to continue.

In addition to developing your beginner's mindset, there are long-term benefits to learning new skills in preparation for your homestead. Learning can keep you healthy and flexible, and boost your happiness. Dennis Buttimer, a health and wellness coach, reveals in a study that while it was once thought that your brain can only change and reshape itself when you are young, there is a consensus among psychologists that your brain continues to reshape itself as you age (Piedmont Healthcare, 2021). Engaging your brain by learning new skills will reshape the way your brain functions and thinks about things. Staying focused, learning quickly, or critically thinking about a problem can be relearned, and your brain can become more receptive to what was once challenging. Learning new skills can also drastically improve your mood; it's no secret that when you learn and master a new skill you are flooded with a sense of accomplishment and fulfillment. In a 2021 article, Buttimer notes that while you may not feel euphoric all the time, constantly learning new skills can boost your general levels of happiness and well-being (Piedmont Healthcare, 2021). While you may have no experience homesteading and all of the tasks are new to you, that is certainly not a reason to avoid it. If homesteading is appealing to you, begin planning! Learning new skills and holding yourself accountable for completing tasks will boost your overall well-being exponentially.

THE BENEFITS OF CREATING YOUR OWN HOMESTEAD

With the Beginner's and Homesteader's mindset in your pocket, let's talk about all the ways that homesteading can benefit your life. I have been homesteading for a decade at this point, and the benefits that homesteading has brought to my life are immeasurable. There are countless opportunities to make homesteading work for the lifestyle that you want, ways to make money in a sustainable and eco-friendly way, and psychological benefits to being around nature. The best tip that I can give a homesteading beginner is to learn what makes you feel grateful. For me, this took some adjustment, but I found that I was grateful for the opportunity to be around nature and to engage my family in that lifestyle. Living with a sense of gratitude has been studied, and demonstrates a deeper sense of fulfillment and happiness. In a Forbes article by psychotherapist Amy Morin, she states that being grateful when you start any journey can improve your existing relationships, improve your physical and mental health, improve your feelings of empathy, improve your self-esteem, and even improve your sleep.

While I can't tell you the best style of homesteading to fit into your life, if you are considering it, approaching the process with a focus on being grateful will make a ton of difference. Feeling grateful, no matter what stage of the process you are in, can dramatically improve your chances of success. I will dig much deeper into the practical skills and tips for starting your first homestead, but it is vital to me that you feel a sense of connectedness and gratefulness when starting the journey. At the end of the day, changing the daily routines of your life to be more centered around nature and growth are central to starting a homestead. The practical skills will follow with much more ease once a sense of confidence in the emotional process has been established.

The Gift of Nature

I am sure that you have heard people say that there are countless benefits to being outside and with nature. While these statements may feel empty, there are real scientific inquiries that have been conducted into the effect that nature can have on our lives. Nature can provide countless medical and mental health benefits such as improving memory and concentration, immune system function, healing abilities, happiness, weight loss, vitamin D production, and reducing symptoms of aging, stress, and depression. Nature's ability to heal and restore can not be emphasized enough.

Taking a walk and being outside in nature has been proven to improve memory and concentration at an incredibly high rate. In a University of Michigan study, subjects were told a series of numbers and asked to repeat them backwards to a researcher. One group was asked to do this after taking a walk around a park, another group was asked to do this after walking around a city block. The study showed that people who were walking amongst nature scored 20% higher on the memory test than did the people who were walking around the city block (Berman et al., 2008). In an additional study, the test was replicated, but instead of walking around nature, the subjects were asked to view pictures of nature and pictures of a city. Again, the results confirmed that people who viewed nature scored better on memory tests than did people who were looking at a city block.

Being in nature can also improve your concentration. We have *directed attention* and *involuntary attention*. In a study conducted by Stephen Kaplan, a researcher and professor of psychology at the University of Michigan, he found that by reducing the *directed attention* that we require by living in a city and constantly being overstimulated, we can improve our *involuntary attention*. This theory is called the Attention Restoration Theory. Directed attention is what we use to process stimuli and short-term memory. Involuntary attention is the instinctual attention that we use for survival. When people live in a city, there is constant stimulus that takes up our directed attention, but when we live in nature or a more rural setting, our directed attention is much less required, and our ability to concentrate increases. Taking a break from the dense stimulus that urban centers offer us can vastly improve our memory and concentration (Kaplan, 1995).

When you begin working on your homestead, you will be moving your body a lot. Depending upon your lifestyle before beginning your homesteading journey, you are likely to lose weight and maintain more lean muscle. Simply by moving around more in nature, you will naturally lose the stubborn weight that you may have. However, studies also show that being in a higher altitude environment can also lead to weight loss. Depending upon where you decide to place your homestead, a higher altitude location could do wonders for weight loss. When people are at higher altitudes, a low form of hypobaric hypoxia may occur. This occurrence happens when the body is deprived of oxygen because the air is thinner at higher altitudes. At a high rate, this can cause health issues in some people, but at lower rates, hypobaric hypoxia can stimulate weight loss and appetite suppression. In a German study, the researchers took 20 overweight subjects to a high-altitude lodge and observed them for a week. The subjects, on average, lost three pounds and maintained the weight loss well after leaving the high altitude lodge. Being outside and active, in general, can definitely lead to weight loss, if that is your goal; however you may also consider finding a homestead property at a slightly higher altitude than you are used to in order to improve your weight-loss gains.

There are also incredible benefits to healing and vitamin D production from being out in nature. In a 2010 publication of the Harvard Health Letter, written by Harvard Medical students, the researchers confirmed that natural sunlight can improve the healing speed in the body and reduce pain from injuries. Our body releases hormones that repair and replenish our internal systems, but for some people, this process can happen irregularly. By spending time outside, it was observed that the hormones responsible for pain management and healing were boosted and regularly circulated throughout the body. Natural sunlight also boosts vitamin D production in the body. Vitamin D is essential for the absorption of other vitamins that your body processes from food and for preventing adverse health events. In the Harvard studies, subjects demonstrated a lower need for pain medication and a lower risk of some cancers, osteoporosis, and heart attacks after daily exposure to natural sunlight.

Being outside has also been shown to be vital for a longer and healthier life. Many people are predisposed to different health issues and we all experience the symptoms of aging. However, by extending the time you spend outside daily, you can mitigate some of these symptoms. In a seven-year study of elderly people, it was observed that the subjects had significantly fewer health issues as a result of spending time outside. For the subjects that went outside daily, they saw a reduction in body aches, sleep problems, incontinence, and many other symptoms that are associated with age. When we spend time in the sun, many health benefits are conferred onto us and the regulation of hormones in our bodies is more consistent. Even if we aren't entering old age, spending time outside can also decrease the risk of adverse health events or symptoms of aging.

A reduction of stress and symptoms of depression, and an increase in happiness, can also be found by spending more time in nature. While there may be times that planning and designing your homestead will feel stressful, taking time outside can drastically reduce stress and stress-related responses. Ecological psychologist Judith Heerwagen claims that, as a result of spending time outside, your heart rate will lower, leading to a reduction of stress. There are many adverse health events that can be tied to high stress and higher heart rates. It is important to find areas where you can destress, and being outside is definitely one of them. Heerwagen also claims that due to the biological identification that we have with nature as a result of evolution, we instinctively respond positively to natural surroundings. There is a sense of protection and comfort that can be found in being outdoors. Those stable and comforting feelings can ease the symptoms of depression. Generally speaking, being outside will create a happier version of you. There are countless accounts of people feeling happier in the summer when they have more access to the outdoors. In a Finnish study on happiness levels as a result of being outside, the researchers found that, regardless of where you are, being outside and close to nature will reduce your cortisol levels, the stress hormones in the brain, and improve your overall well-being.

2

YOUR OPTIONS

*T*here are many options to consider when you are planning for your homestead. One of the first is "Where in the world are you?" There are different zones, called hardiness zones, that the United States Department of Agriculture (USDA) has laid out to show what type of planting and gardening will be the most successful in those areas.

Hardiness zones consider the high and low temperatures in Fahrenheit, as well as the aridity and humidity of where you are, to determine the best crops to grow. The temperatures associated with each zone are determined by the annual minimum winter temperatures. Knowing your hardiness zone will be imperative to understanding the limitations that you can have on your homestead. Some fruits, vegetables, and flowers will grow great in some climates and terribly in others. It is also important to note whether you want to grow annual plants or perennial plants. Annual plants are those that germinate, flower, seed, and die within one season. Perennial plants are typically able to survive and protect themselves from cold temperatures so that they can re-emerge in the next season.

Both annual and perennial plants have one season that they prefer to bloom in. Taking all of these factors into account when you are planning your homestead will lead to paramount success for your harvests. While the following sections have a list of possible crops to grow in each zone, there are many more. If you are curious about a crop that was not listed, be sure to research that specific crop and its needs.

HARDINESS ZONES

Cold Climates

The hardiness zones for the colder climates are zone 1 through zone 4. The first four zones are largely the coldest and most difficult places to grow crops. If you can thrive in colder climates, these zones are perfect for you.

Zone 1

Zone 1 sees winters that are typically between -60 °F to -50 °F and is really reserved for the Arctic Coast, which includes Alaska and Northern Canada. While there are few crops that can withstand the coldest climates, there are certainly some native crops that are worth investing your time into. Annuals can be a great option during the growing season as they don't need to sustain themselves during the coldest part of the year.

For some great annual vegetables, choose broccoli, cabbage, kale, radishes, spinach, sweet peas, and tomatoes. If your area reaches summer temperatures of 60 to 70°F lettuce will thrive, but without these summer highs, it may be worth skipping. Some great herbs to grow are basil, mint, oregano, rosemary, and thyme. All of these crops will serve you well in harsher climates and yield great results as you won't have to worry about them surviving through the winter.

Some great perennial vegetable crops are beans, potatoes, and sweet potatoes. It is important to note that with any potatoes, if the roots are not intact and don't remain buried, they will not grow in the next season. Some fruit trees that will continue to bear fruits season after season are chokecherry trees, apple trees, and haskap or honeyberries. The apple trees that will do best are End apples, Fort Mac Mac apples, and September Ruby apples, but many other varieties will grow too. The only winter hardy herb to grow is chives, while some of the best flowers are arrowheads, delphinium, goldenrods, sunflowers, lily of the valleys, oxeye daisies, and yarrow.

Zone 2

The growing season for both zone 1 and 2 is from April to September. Many of the previously mentioned crops can thrive in colder climates and have the ability to survive until the next growing season, but there are more options in zone 2 Zone 2 is the very northern part of the continental United States, including Colorado, Maine, Montana, New York, Washington, and Wyoming, and extends up into Canada. Zone 2 minimum winter temperatures are between -50 °F to -40 °F.

Annual vegetables that are great for zone 2, along with all the vegetables for zone 1, are carrots, mustard greens, onions, parsnips, and swiss chard. Carrots and parsnips will need to be planted as an annual crop the first season that you plant them, but after the first season, so long as the roots are intact, they become biennial crops and will regrow the following season. There are also many different onion varieties that can be grown as perennials but it is best to grow them as annual crops.

There are many perennial fruit trees that you can grow in zone 2, but a few great ones are Brookgold, Fofonodd, and Pembina plum trees, Fall Red, Minnesota 1734, Norkent, and Parkland apple trees, chokecherry trees, and Korean pine trees. These are all native to North America and can survive the winter without withering and ceasing to produce fruit in the following season. Take care to plant these trees at least 15 feet apart for large varieties to ensure their success.

There are also many perennial flowers that can be grown, including bleeding hearts, monkshood, penstemon, poppies, primroses, sea holly, and violets. If you want a garden that is vibrant in different violet colors, consider planting them annually, as this will increase the chance of a beautiful medley of purple flowers. Juniper shrubs, hyssop, and Turkestan roses are also winter-hardy perennials worth considering.

Zone 3

We are still not out of the cold yet. Zone 3 has minimum winter temperatures of -40 °F to -30 °F. The states included are parts of Michigan, New Hampshire, South Dakota, Vermont, and Wyoming.

Zone 3 also extends across the southern strip of provinces in Canada.

The annual vegetables that are great for zone 3 are celery, cucumbers, and summer and winter squash. All of these crops may be able to survive for longer growing seasons or have perennial varieties, but in zone 3 it is best to plant these as annuals. Annual herbs for zone 3 are caraway, English chamomile, French sorrel, garlic, and parsley. Caraway is a biennial herb that won't produce flowers in the first season, but will return in the second growing season if they are well taken care of. English chamomile and French sorrel are considered perennials in zones 4 through 11 but in zone 3 it is best to grow them as annuals. The best flowers to grow as annuals are salvia and spurge, as both flowers will have great yields.

The best perennial vegetable to grow is asparagus. This cold-hardy vegetable can grow annually for up to 15 years after the first growing season if treated with care. Among the fruit trees that are both native and cold-hardy enough to grow perennially are Cupid and Evans cherry trees, Dolgo crabapple trees, Early Fold, Golden Spice pear trees, Goodland and Sweet Sixteen apple trees, Toka and Waneta plum trees, and Westcott apricot trees. Perennial herbs to grow are catnip, horseradish, and peppermint. I particularly suggest growing catnip, because there is an incredible return on investment for this herb. The perennial flowers that are best are alpine rockcress, aster, blanket flower, liatris, snow-in-summer, Virginia bluebells, and wallflower. These flowers will make your garden come alive during the growing season and you won't need to replant them in the following growing seasons.

Zone 4

The last of the coldest climates is zone 4, which reaches minimum winter temperatures of -30 °F to -20 °F and extends through the southernmost part of the Canadian provinces and the upper northern

United States. The best states for zone 4 homesteading are Colorado, Idaho, Iowa, and Nebraska.

As we move into more moderate temperatures, there are more opportunities to grow perennial crops over annual crops. However, the best annual vegetables to grow are melons, okra, and pumpkins. All of these crops will deliver great yields when cared for, and the pumpkins can be a great return on investment during the fall season. An annual herb worth mentioning is garden sage. Sage will thrive in zone 4 as an annual herb, but beyond zone 4, in zones 5 through 8, garden sage is considered a perennial herb.

The best perennial vegetable is eggplant. Eggplants are incredibly cold-hardy, and while their growth cycle significantly slows during the winter months, you will not need to replant the crop. The fruit trees that can withstand the harsher winters and are native are Aiderman and Ewing blue plum trees; Alexander, Railroad and Trent apple trees; Nova and Summercrisp pear trees; Buartnut—a variety of walnut; and Butternut. Some herbs and flowers that you can plant as perennials are angelicas, bee balm, coneflower, daylily, hostas, iris, lemon balm, mountain mint, phlox, thyme, and winter savory. These herbs and flowers will have your garden looking like a dream during the growing season and will save you precious time the following season as they regrow on their own.

Moderate Climates

Zone 5

Moving into the more moderate climates, zone 5 reaches minimum winter temperatures of -20 °F to -30 °F. Some of the best areas to find farms are the southern border between Canada and the United States. The southernmost parts of Alberta, British Columbia, Manitoba, Ontario, and Saskatchewan all have farmable land as well. The states that have large zone 5 areas are Colorado, Idaho, Iowa,

Michigan, Montana, Nebraska, all of New England, New York, South Dakota, Washington, Wisconsin, and Wyoming.

The best annual vegetables are kale, lettuce, radishes, spinach, and winter greens. Kale can be grown as a perennial or biennial in warmer zones, but for zone 5, kale is best grown as an annual crop. A lovely annual flower that will bring vibrance to any zone 5 garden are Black-Eyed Susans. Black-Eyed Susans are considered vine flowers and can be used to decorate the outside of fences or walls with beautiful bright orange flowers. There are also many perennial trees that are worth growing, including Honeycrisp and Pink Lady apple trees, Harrow Delight and Warren pear trees, native pawpaw trees, Snow Beauty peach trees, and Superior plum trees. All of these trees are native to zone 5 and will thrive during the growing season and protect themselves during the colder months. Perennial herbs that are good to grow are mint, calamint, and lavender. As a general rule, all varieties of mint are incredibly cold-hardy and worth the investment if your homestead experiences colder temperatures. They are a delicious herb to keep in a kitchen garden and the return on your investment is second to none. Lastly, some great flowers to grow perennially are baptisia, campanula, and Russian sage. Russian sage is particularly cold-hardy and can be grown in zones 4 through 9.

Zone 6

Zone 6 sees minimum winter temperatures of -10 °F to 0 °F and starts with longer spring and fall cycles. The states for homesteading in zone 6 are Arizona, California, Colorado, Idaho, Illinois, Kansas, Kentucky, Missouri, Nevada, New Mexico, Ohio, Oregon, Pennsylvania, Utah, and Washington. In Canada, the west coast of British Columbia and the southernmost tip of Ontario have areas that are perfect for homesteading. When considering what to grow, the best annual vegetables are bush beans, butter lettuce, melons, tomatoes, and winter squash. Bush beans should be treated with special care in the earliest part of their growing cycle to ensure that they regrow in the next season, but for the sake of working smarter, bush beans are best as annuals. Some annual herbs to grow are borage, coriander, dill, chamomile, and oregano. All of these herbs are perfect for a kitchen garden and can be used in your daily cooking if treated with care. Two flowers that will grow annually are sunflowers and floribunda roses. The roses have incredibly long blooming periods and will bloom from the beginning of spring to the end of fall. They are definitely a great addition to a beautiful flower garden. The perennial fruit trees that you should consider are Jefferson plum trees; Late Crawford, Loring, Madison, and Nectar peach trees; and Red Globe nectarine trees. These fruit trees are great in warmer climates as well, but zone 6 is the start of their desired temperature range. Perennial flowers that are perfect for zone 6 are flowering ferns, Japanese bottlebrushes, Lady's mantle, and sedum.

Zone 7

Moving into even more moderate climates, the opportunities for perennial crops begin to expand. There is much less risk of cold-damaged plants in zones 7 through 9, so the chances of multiple-year harvests become higher. The minimum winter temperatures in zone 7 are 0 °F to 10 °F. Zone 7 includes Arkansas, North Carolina, Oklahoma, Tennessee, and Texas, but does not include Colorado, Idaho, Illinois, or Ohio. The only place for zone 7 homesteading in Canada is the west coast of British Columbia.

Annual vegetables that are perfect for zone 7 are arugula and turnips. The herb marjoram is also grown as an annual crop in zone 7, but it becomes a perennial crop after zone 9. Two annual flowers that you can grow are forget-me-nots and four o'clocks. Both of these flowers are particularly delicate and need a lot of maintenance if you want to see the second harvest in the following season. The best perennial vegetables are hot and sweet peppers, however, it is important to note that peppers will need protection from the frost during winter. Covering or repotting and moving them into your greenhouse are your best options.

There are many different fruit trees that will produce yearly harvests for many years which include Bing, Rainier Sweet, and Stella cherry trees; Cortland, Fuji, and Granny Smith apple trees; Moorpark and Scout apricot trees; Blue Java banana trees; Contender peach trees; Fuyu persimmon trees; Ozark plum trees; Parker pear trees; Red Gold nectarine trees; Turkey fig-trees; and pawpaw trees. You may also consider mulberry or elderberry bushes as well. Some herbs to grow in a perennial kitchen garden are feverfew, rue, sage, and tarragon. All of these are hardy enough to brace for the cooler temperatures in the winter and return in the spring. Some perennial flowers that you might grow are butterfly weed, Candytuft, chrysanthemums, clematis, painted daisies, and peonies. The clematis is considered a vine flower and can also be used as a gorgeous decoration for your fences or walls.

Zone 8

The minimum winter temperatures in zone 8 are 10 °F to 20 °F and there are many areas in the United States that are suited for zone 8 farming. Zone 8 includes Alabama, Arkansas, California, Florida, Louisiana, Nevada, New Mexico, North Carolina, Oregon, South Carolina, and Washington. The rest of the hardiness zones see minimum temperatures that do not exist in Canada. Annual crops that are best for zone 8 farming are cantaloupe, lettuce, field peas, okra, tomatoes, and watermelon. A great annual flower to grow in zone 8 is lantana. Again, a great perennial crop is sweet and hot peppers, but they will need protection during the colder months. The fruit trees are endless, but some of the best options are Anna and Gala apple trees, Marsh and Ruby grapefruit trees, Alma fig-trees, Bryan apricot trees, Clementine tangerine trees, Jujube trees, Kumquat and

Limequat trees, Meyer lemon trees, Montmorency cherry trees, Washington orange trees, and all of the previously mentioned peach and plum trees. For herbs, Bay laurel, marjoram, Mexican oregano, rosemary, and sage will all thrive, while some lovely flowers would be Asiatic lilies, Hardy Geraniums, Mexican petunias, and phlox. The Mexican petunias can also be grown perennially through zone 11.

Zone 9

The last of the moderate climate zones, zone 9, sees minimum winter temperatures of 20 °F to 30 °F. Zone 9 is identical to zone 8 in the United States, but it excludes Washington and Oregon. Broccoli, Brussels sprouts, cabbage, cauliflower, and spinach are great annual vegetables to grow here. Basil is the only herb that needs to be grown annually, while Black-Eyed Susans, Canna lilies, and zinnias also need to be grown as annual flowers. Some perennial tree options are avocado trees, calamondin trees (a type of citrus), giant pomelo trees, hardy kiwi trees, Mandarin and Trifoliate orange trees, olive trees and bushes, passionfruit trees, and starfruit trees. Some perennial herbs are chives, marjoram, mint, bay laurel, coriander, and lemon thyme. Three of the best flowers are dahlias, rhododendrons, and wisteria.

Dry Climates

Zone 10

Going into the drier climates, zone 10 sees minimum winter temperatures of 30 °F to 40 °F, so there aren't many annual crops that need to be protected from the cold and harsh winters. Zone 10 and 11 are the driest and warmest zones. These zones include California, Nevada, Arizona, and Texas. An annual garden in zone 10 will be able to grow melons, jicama, peanuts, tomatillos, euonymus shrubs, and floss flowers. The best perennial vegetable to grow is Malabar spinach. Some great fruit trees to grow are Allspice trees, Apple guava trees, Carica papaya trees, Jackfruit trees, Soursop trees, June plum trees, and Dwarf Cavendish banana trees. Curry leaf, galangal, ginger, Mexican tarragon, and miracle fruits are all great herbs to choose as well. The Mexican tarragon requires a lot of attention if you want to maintain it as a perennial crop, otherwise, it is perfectly acceptable to grow it annually. The miracle fruits are native to West Africa and require a lot of shade. These crops are typically seeded on specialty farms but they are definitely manageable for a homestead. The best flowers to grow as perennials in zone 10 are agave, African lilies, aloe vera, Delta Maidenhair ferns, geraniums, hummingbird mint, ornamental onions, and Peruvian lilies.

Zone 11

Zone 10 and 11 share the same geographical regions in the United States, however, zone 11 sees minimum winter temperatures of 40 °F to 50 °F. Some annual vegetables to grow are beets, cabbage, carrots, radishes, sweet peas, and Swiss Chard. There are many variations of sweet peas that can be grown perennially, depending on the amount of time you are willing to commit to maintenance. A great perennial vegetable to grow is kale.

Some fruit trees that are best are Jaboticaba trees, Macadamia trees, Mango trees, Moringa trees, Natal plum trees, and Seagrape trees or bushes. Your herb garden can include chives, mint, basil, lemongrass, thyme, Mexican oregano, and Kangaroo paw. Kangaroo paw has a five year life plan and is native to Australia. Some perennial flowers to grow in are bougainvillea, Drumstick Alliums, begonias, and Ponytail Palms. The bougainvillea is a vine flower that is great for a decorative garden.

Tropical Climates

Zone 12 and 13

The last set of hardiness zones are the tropical climates. Zones 12 and 13 are reserved for the most tropical and humid areas of the United States. These zones include Florida, Louisiana, Puerto Rico, and Hawaii. Zone 12 has minimum winter temperatures of 50 °F to 60 °F, and zone 13 has minimum winter temperatures of 60 °F to 70 °F. Bush beans, eggplant, summer squash, borage, and cilantro are the annual plants to grow these zones. Perennial vegetables that are great in zone 12 and 13 are hot peppers and tomatoes as they won't need much protection in the colder months. The fruit trees to grow in zone 12 and 13 are African apricot trees, Ackee trees, African breadfruit trees, Alupag trees, Amazon tree-grape, Bignay trees, Black pepper trees, Imbee trees, Tropical almond trees, and Jaca Olive trees. Similarly, the best perennial flowers for both zone 12 and 13 are Cannacaeae, Coastaceae, Bird-of-Paradise, Heliconia, Marantaceae, Musaceae, and Zingiberaceae.

PERMACULTURE ZONES

Permaculture stands for *permanent agriculture* and it is a system of "zones" that have nothing to do with temperature. Permaculture zones are manageable chunks of your homestead where different activities and maintenance are performed. Splitting your homestead into manageable areas will allow you to feel less overwhelmed and more organized as you approach homesteading. There are also large ecological benefits to laying out your homestead with permaculture zones. This style of designing your homestead considers the entire process that you'd like to have and allows you to plan for all of it. If you are still only considering homesteading, it is a great practice to find a bit of land that you may be interested in and try out the following permaculture layout strategies to see if this would be a manageable undertaking for you.

To begin laying out the permaculture zones on a plot of land, you will first need to print out an aerial map of the property. This is a super easy first step, because Google Maps and Google Earth both have aerial features that you can pull screenshots from. They also offer features so that you can see the topography of the land you are working with. This will become important later down the line for storage and running water. Once you have a printed map of your farm, mark out the large structures and natural features on the property. Mark out any buildings, large trees that will not be cut down, and any natural water sources. Marking these things on the map will help you find a central location to branch out from.

After you have marked out the structures, make a list of all of the elements and activities that you'd like to have on your homestead. I will dig deeper into these options later, but for now, what are some of the elements that you would ideally like to have on your homestead? Are you interested in keeping bees or maybe having large plots of land to grow annual plants? Once the list is complete, note how much time it would take you during the week to attend to all of these elements. Let's say that you want to have a large plot of land for growing annual plants—during the day or each week, how much time will you need to allot to watering, nurturing, and harvesting the crops?—you should first develop a time breakdown and establish which permaculture zone each element will be in.

Now that you have a comprehensive list of all of the activities and elements you'd like to have and how much time each element is allotted, you should plot out the different zones. There are five permaculture zones listed below with some examples of what could go into each to consider when you are plotting your design. This is the design phase, and you will probably scrap many designs before you find one that works best for you. Continue this process until you feel confident with the design of your homestead. The size of your property will also greatly impact the layout. If you are on an urban or smaller homestead, you may only be able to fit a couple of zones onto your property. That is totally fine! There are many different styles of homesteading, and so long as you have a permaculture layout that works for your area, you will be golden.

After you have gone through the versions of each permaculture zone that works for you, list out the activities that you would perform in a week. I would consider doing this for the height of a growing season and for the winter season when you are spending more time indoors. List out each zone and how much time you will spend there over the course of the week. If you are struggling to fit everything in or you are not able to maintain everything on your homestead at your comfort level, I suggest either moving elements into different zones or expanding the zones. It is possible that due to time restrictions you may not be able to get over a zone for maintenance that needs to be performed twice a week, so move that element into a different zone. There is a lot of flexibility in this process and I recommend trying several different layouts so that you find what suits your needs the best. When I was designing my first permaculture zones, I really wanted to prioritize having a kitchen garden, an area that could be used to dine outside, a place to keep bees, and a larger area on the property to grow crops. I knew that the walk from my back door to the larger crop area could be no longer than 5 minutes or I would struggle to get out there regularly. I used the permaculture design strategies to inform my layout so that my kitchen garden and outside dining area were adjacent to my house and left some room for decorative landscaping. About a two minute walk from my door, nestled between the kitchen garden and the crops, I place an area for beehives. These strategies for designing the layout of your property are flexible and accommodating to exactly what you want to have on your farm.

Permaculture Zone 0

Zone 0 is inside your house. I include this zone because it is important to consider what processes you'd like to keep inside your house to support the maintenance of your homestead. There are many different styles of homesteads and what you keep immediately inside your house can support your daily activities. If you are starting an urban homestead and you only have 2 or 3 zones, it may be important to keep your composting bin inside your house. If you have a large off-the-grid homestead, it may be worthwhile to keep a tractor in your garage so that you have an easier time traveling through the zones. Whatever your case may be, don't skip planning what will make your life easier in zone 0.

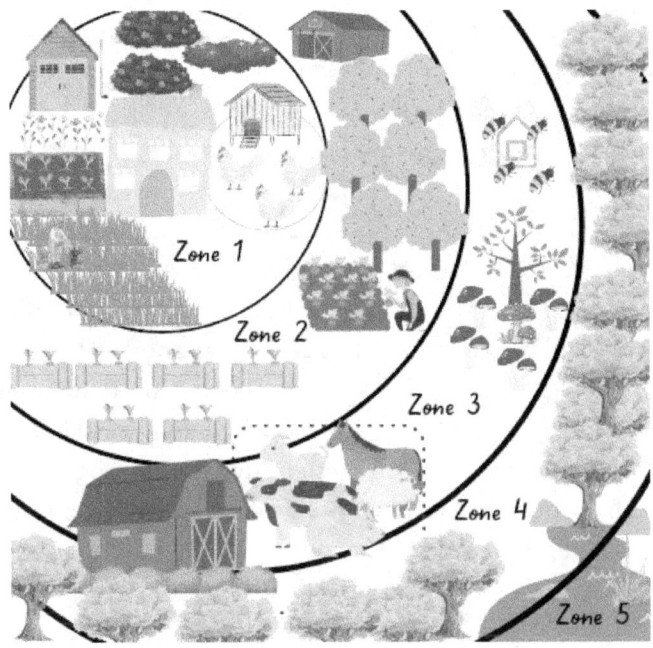

Permaculture Zone 1

Zone 1 is the domestic zone. This is the area immediately outside your house. Zone 1 is checked and maintained daily. There are many options for what to have immediately outside of your house, and again, this is dependent on the type of homestead you wish to culti-vate. If you are starting a family homestead, it may be worthwhile to have an eco-lawn, a play area for the kids, a kitchen garden, and an outdoor seating area. The eco-lawn is something that I highly recom-mend, as it is a great space for kids to play and potentially a leisure area when the day is done. The same goes for the outdoor seating area. If your homestead is somewhere that gets temperate nights, hang some lights out there and have dinner with the family. The kitchen garden is also great for family-style homesteads. The kitchen garden can be a small herb and annual crops garden. Having a kitchen garden in zone 1 will mean that it is easily accessible for mealtimes and you can keep an eye on it every day to ensure that it is thriving.

If you are not starting a family homestead, but instead have a little extra room for zone 1, consider planting small fruit trees, berry bushes, or aesthetically pleasing seasonal flowers. You will be in this area daily, so I suggest that you make it as inviting as possible. Zone 1 should be an area that you want to be in, as it will start and end your day, every day. Regardless of the style of zone 1, be sure to have a small shed in the area with tools specifically for maintaining zones 0 and 1. There will be room for a larger shed in another zone for main-tenance on a larger homestead, but having the tools that you will need for the maintenance of zones 0 and 1 immediately available will make repairs that much easier. When you are in the planning phase, the list of things that you want to have is essential to determine what zone they are in. The golden rule for zone 1 is if you are going to need access to it daily, it goes in zone 1.

Permaculture Zone 2

Zone 2 is the home orchard. This is a zone that will also receive daily maintenance and cultivation chores. It is important that zone 2 is easily accessible and doesn't require you to walk a long distance to reach. Again, as a daily maintenance zone, it is crucial that you make it there every day, so when you are laying out the farm, be sure to put this in an accessible location. Some ideas for what to put in zone 2 are fruit trees, berry bushes or shrubs, perennial vegetables, pollinator flowers, small animal coops, farm compost and mulch bins, and the main shed. It is great to have your food forest in zone 2 as it will require regular attention. Having the fruits, berries, and perennial vegetable garden here will give you daily access to the area so you can ensure that the main crops on your farm are thriving. Zone 2 is also an area to put small animal coops because they, too, will require daily attention. Chicken, rabbit, or duck coops are great for this zone.

As zone 2 requires daily maintenance, unlike zones 3-5, it is a great midpoint to place the main shed for tools that you only need to maintain the larger areas of your homestead.

Permaculture Zone 3

Zone 3 is the farming zone. This area will only be visited a handful of times a week and doesn't require daily maintenance. If you are finding that you will need to visit an area that you are placing in zone 3 more than three times a week, move it up to zone 2. Some examples of things that belong in zone 3 are a non-regular perennial vegetable garden, a staple crop garden, large animals that don't require daily attention, beehives, mushroom cultivation, and coppice groves. The non-regular perennial vegetable garden and the staple crop garden are for perennials that don't require daily maintenance and can be watered and cultivated every couple of days. These crops will vary based on where your homestead is, but the main crops that are great for this area are wheat and potatoes as they require minimal maintenance and will continue to grow each season without replanting. Large, grazing animals and bee hives can also be kept in zone 3, and have benefits that will be discussed later. For now, the important thing to note is that they are not high-need aspects and with some self-sustaining systems they will thrive on their own.

Beyond functional homesteading structures that can be put in place in zone 3, I advise leaving it open to the natural ecosystem that surrounds your farm. Mushroom harvesting and a coppice grove are great for this reason. If you allow the natural vegetation in the area to take root and thrive here, you will be able to leverage the growth that takes place naturally. Coppice groves are created by cutting down an area that is densely packed with trees to their stumps and allowing them to regrow. This allows you to have a stronger hand in assisting the natural habitat around your homestead to thrive.

Tree management is great for native flowers and mushrooms to thrive, but when the trees are too densely packed, these native plants will not grow. After cutting the trees down to the stump, you should make sure to leave some of the larger branches attached. When cutting the larger branches, cut the ends of the branches at an angle away from the stump so that water can run down the nubs and water the trees. Depending on the growth cycle of the tree, this cycle can be repeated to promote regrowth and ecosystem balance. The cut-off from the trees can be used in building and warming your home. Establishing a coppice cycle is certainly a hefty task that can be very time-consuming depending on the size of your property, but the cycle will pay off tenfold. The promotion of native plants and animals in your area will develop in a couple of seasons and the tree growth will be manageable.

Permaculture Zone 4

Zone 4 is the forage zone. This zone requires very minimal care and it is an area perfect for acquiring resources and utilizing the natural ecosystems to your benefit. There are also opportunities to replenish this area. Some examples of activities for zone 4 are hunting, gathering native plants, selective grazing, fishing, and harvesting wood from larger trees or even extending the coppice grove. This zone is a great place to begin learning the natural patterns in your area and utilizing their benefits while giving back to the land. Hunting, gathering, coppicing, and fishing all benefit you as the homesteader, but they also allow for practices that will manage the ecological systems around you so that they can thrive. It is a great practice to allow your larger animals to selectively graze in zone 4. This is not only a cost-effective source of food for your animals, but it can also prevent wildfires.

Permaculture Zone 5

The last zone is the wilderness zone. Zone 5 requires minimal-to-no management. This zone, more so than zone 4, is largely for observation. In zone 5 you are able to truly observe the ecological patterns of the land around your homestead. Observation can be pivotal to improving your homesteading practices as well. You may find that a stream or the way that the sun reaches certain areas can improve the layout of the interior zones.

However, it is important to note that beginning a homestead that has enough area for a zone 5 is rare. Many homesteads won't be large enough to have a wilderness zone due to the limitations of a given property. It is useful, if you have room for a zone 5, to first consider it a zone 4 so that you can properly cultivate the area. It is unwise to ignore this area, because that would ignore past interactions on that land. Any debris or ecological imbalances that may have taken place here should be addressed so that you can have a thriving ecosystem outside of your homestead. Considering the wilderness zone, a zone 4 can be great at first and you will slowly be able to transition this area to zone 5 as you feel confident in your interventions.

There are no absolutes when starting a permaculture-based homestead. It is very unlikely that all of these zones will sit perfectly in one place or another. Designing with a permaculture lens will mean managing your wishes for your homestead with the reality and capability of the land that you have. At this stage in your homesteading journey, planning out your permaculture zones and determining the right things to have may feel overwhelming. If you are interested in taking a deep dive into the nuanced details of permaculture design, beyond a general overview, Oregon State University has a free course on its platform that details every step in the permaculture process.

3

WHICH HOMESTEAD STYLE IS RIGHT FOR YOU?

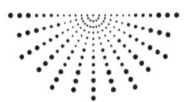

URBAN HOMESTEADS

$\mathcal{U}$rban homesteading can be the start of your journey to a larger homestead or it can be a way to live more sustainably in a big city. There are as many choices for urban homesteading as there are for a more traditional rural homestead. Urban homesteads can be small gardens in an apartment or tiny plots of land in your backyard. If you are someone who is utilizing an urban homestead to transition to a larger homestead in the future, this style of homesteading can be perfect for practicing the skills you will need when you move onto a larger plot of land. However, if this is not the case, there are countless benefits to urban homesteading: you can increase the quality and security of food for you and the people you live with, waste less food, save money on foods you would otherwise buy, and conserve energy and water to decrease your carbon footprint.

The options for urban homesteading can take many different forms. Your garden can be a small one that is just for you and your family or you could participate in a community garden where you are developing homesteading practices alongside other people who are passionate about farming. I will dive deeper into the different styles of urban gardening that you can employ as part of your urban homesteading journey, but for now, it is important to note that the skills that you will need for any homestead are applicable regardless of size.

So where do you start when you want to begin an urban homestead? The first place to start is with a garden. Starting your journey with a garden will allow you to determine the other sustainable needs that you will need to incorporate. The first step is to determine what type of garden you want. There are a ton of options to choose from for an urban homestead: vertical farm, a hydroponic farm, an aquaponic farm, a container or rooftop farm, or a backyard garden. For each of these, there are space and financial constraints that will need to fit into your current circumstances. If you are living in an apartment, a rooftop or community garden may be a great option. If you have some upfront capital that you can invest into your urban homesteading journey, it may be worth looking into a vertical, hydroponic, or aquaponic farm.

Vertical farms call for stacking your crops on vertical shelving and can be combined with other methods of farming to increase efficiency during grow cycles. The benefits of vertical farms are that they can be placed virtually anywhere. If you have access to a greenhouse, a shipping container, or even a basement, vertical farming can be a great option in increasing your yield and making the most of your space. Additionally, hydroponic and aquaponic farming is a great option for urban farmers. Hydroponic farming calls for no soil, and instead you are able to soak the roots of your crops in water that is saturated with the nutrients that your crops need to thrive. This system is great for conserving water, as you will reuse the water for the crops and can be a great way to practice sustainable farming in a smaller space. Aquaponic farming calls for having crops that are also saturated in water, but instead of adding nutrients to the water, you add fish. The fish produce waste that is essential for plant growth and can be an additional source of income. As the fish mature, you can sell them to subsidize your urban farm. There are many different configurations that can be used when implementing an aquaponic farming style. You can also combine vertical farming with hydroponic or aquaponic farming. These options are perfect for a backyard greenhouse or shipping container. Creativity will be your best friend when you are urban farming so that you can make the most of space.

Once you have decided what type of farm you'd like to have in your urban space, it is time to move on to the next steps: deciding what to grow, getting the tools that you will need, and planting. To decide what crops are the best to grow, refer back to the hardiness zones for outdoor farms. Wherever your urban farm is located, the hardiness zones will inform the best crops to grow outdoors. If you are starting an indoor or greenhouse urban farm, you have a lot more flexibility in what crops you can grow. A temperature-controlled environment affords you a lot more creativity, and if you combine indoor farming with a vertical, hydroponic, or aquaponic farm, there are other steps that you will need to take to ensure that you are picking the best crops for your growing space.

Now that you have an idea of what kind of urban farm you can build and what crops will work best for your space, it is time to invest in tools. If you are starting an outdoor or traditional greenhouse farm where your crops will rely on soil, some of the best starter tools are gardening gloves, a gardening trowel, a gardening dibber, pruning shears, a cultivator, a soil moisture sensor, watering wand or other watering can, rain barrel, shovel, and rake. Having this inventory of tools will make it so that you are never lacking a basic tool to get the job done. With more advanced farming builds, there are more tools worth considering so that you can ensure the best success for your farm.

The last step to starting your urban farm is to start planting! This is probably the most rewarding step in the process for me. I love the ability to get my hands dirty and plan out the growing cycle for each crop. I feel a real sense of control and can watch the growing cycle with a sense of pride. For each urban farming type, the type of care that a crop will need is largely dependent on that crop. Some crops need little to no care while others need a lot. Some fundamental information that you will need about each crop is how much space it will need, the desired pH of the soil or water, how deep to plant the seeds if you are using soil, and how much water it will need. For sunlight, each crop is divided into three categories: full sun, partial sun, and full shade crops. Full sun crops require six to eight hours of sunlight per day, partial sun crops require four to six hours, and full shade crops require two to four hours. In an outdoor farm, you will be restricted in your crop options as your hardiness zone and access to sunlight allows. With a greenhouse or temperature-controlled farm, the sunlight hours can be provided by full-spectrum growing lights and the right temperature.

Some additional steps that you can make when you are starting your urban farm are to invest in some renewable energy resources. A compost bin, water bin, and solar panels are great options if you are looking to conserve energy and water and reduce your carbon footprint. There are multiple options for DIYing your compost bin for an urban farm that I will get into later. There are also many companies that have started selling compact composting bins for smaller living spaces. A water bin is also a great option. They collect rainwater for you to use to water your crops and the water can be recycled depending on the farm type you are using. Plants love rainwater and thrive best when you store and reuse rainwater. It is a great practice to set up water collection bins in different areas around your urban farm. If you are in a larger city, there are many places where rainwater is dumped from gutters, and this water can be collected and used for your crops. If you have a backyard farm, you can set up multiple water bins around your property to maximize your water collection.

Solar panels are another option for urban farmers, and the panels can accomplish so many tasks on your farm that they are definitely worth the consideration. Solar panels can be used to generate solar energy to pump water into your crops depending on your irrigation system, they can be used in greenhouse ventilation systems for extra temperature control, and they can heat the air in your greenhouse to create warmer and more humid climates so that you can grow a wider range of crops. The energy conservation that solar panels can bring to your farm is endless and can be crucial to coming up with creative solutions for a smaller farm.

RURAL HOMESTEADS

There are countless benefits to starting your homesteading journey on a rural farm. Not only are you allotted more space to try different systems on your farm, but you can also reap the benefits of being surrounded by nature. If you are starting your homesteading journey with a rural farm, refer back to the permaculture zones and structure. With a rural farm there is more flexibility to include zones 3 and 4, unlike an urban homestead.

In addition to the permaculture zones, there is a principle called the *scale of permanence* that is worth noting if you are considering a rural homestead. The scale of permanence requires that you understand the local climate, the water fixtures on your property, the access points, the existing structures on the property, and the soil. In order to understand the local climate, refer back to the strategies that I previously mentioned for plotting the permaculture zones on your farm. In addition to the layout that you've created, it is important to understand the temperature, insolation (sun exposure), wind, annual humidity, rainfall, and topography of your property. All of these require you to do some research on your local area. It is no surprise that, as a result of global warming, some of the information about the local climate is sure to either be in flux or there are additional precautions that you will need to take when laying out the structure of your farm. When you are designing the layout of your permaculture zones, there is a function on both Google Maps and Google Earth where you can view the topography of your property. This will become vitally important when you begin to understand the access to water and other permanent features on your homestead. My best piece of advice when accessing the first principle in the scale of permanence is to do a lot of research on the local area as well as your property. You will need to know as much information as you can about the existing natural structures on the farm soil and beneath it.

It may be the case that your property is in a rocky area and there are a lot of large boulders under the main farming area. It is important to get this information, as it will inform you of your next action steps.

The next step is to understand and plot the water fixtures on your property. You will need to know if there are any diversions, swales, terraces, dams, ponds, and or channels on your farm. Diversions are areas where the water runoff has built up or where the rainwater has naturally carved a path on your property. You can either choose to work with the existing structure or reroute the diversion to a different area of the farm. Swales are a structurally strategic rain collection method that you can employ on your farm. Similar to a diversion, a natural swale is a dip in the land that is created by rain runoff. You can strategically place swales on your farm so that they collect water and pump that water into the soil of a neighboring farming plot. This is a great and natural irrigation system that only requires you to maintain the swale. Terraces, dams, ponds, and channels are all examples of other natural water sources on your property that are worth capitalizing on. If you can leverage the natural water features on your farm to water your crops and irrigate the soil, you will drastically reduce some of the costs associated with your homestead.

In order to best utilize the water features on your property, you will need to determine water storage, methods of water harvesting, and how you will divide the water. To determine the water storage that you will need on your farm, you will need to figure out how much stored water you will need to sustain yourself, the crops, and livestock. You will also need to know how much rainfall you will get on average. The calculation to determine how much water you will need to store is one millimeter of rain on one square meter of land equals one liter of water for your farm (1mm of rain on $1m^2$ = 1L of water). This equation will allow you to determine how many water collection methods you will need to employ on your farm. I suggest investing in rainwater collection bins, however, there are other strategies to try. If you find a water source that is on a higher elevation than your main farm area, it is a great practice to use plastic piping and gravity to water your crops or drain the water into a collection bin.

This transitions us into water harvesting methods. I strongly recommend having a well on your farm, but don't do it yourself when you are just starting out. Buy a property that already has a well on it! If you can afford it, hire a professional to dig for an aquifer. Another option for water collection, if you have a water source on higher elevation, is to employ the use of tanks. There are many tanks specifically geared towards homesteaders that can be placed in water features to assist in pumping water out of the water feature towards crops or livestock. However, this isn't to say that you should burn through all the water that you can get your hands on. Dividing your water is imperative to preserving the natural features of your farm. It is important to spread the rainwater that you collect evenly across your farm. Utilize swales and other water disbursement methods. Once you have established the flow of water around your farm, roads and fences are to follow. The scale of permanence is important to follow when designing the layout of your farm because some things can only be placed once.

The next step is to define your access points. These are roads, paths, and fencing. Permanent features on the property need to be established early into the process as they are very difficult to change later on down the line. Changing these permanent features can also prove to be incredibly labor and cost intensive. Access points should be influenced by the climate, topography, and water supply that you have established. When establishing roads, it is best to consider the higher elevation between the water lines that you have created. This will ensure that the roads do not flood and that they will drain when it rains. Consider the zones that you have established on the map of your property. Each zone should have some sort of subdivision of fences to maintain the property. These will become particularly important if you introduce animals to your homestead. In the beginning, it is important to consider the more permanent fences that you will need to build. The fences can be traditional wire or wooden fences, or they can be natural fences like trees or hedges—a windbreak around your land can also be a great choice. The importance of subdividing the zones can instill a sense of management and cohesion in your homestead so that it is clear which areas serve which purpose. Consider the roads, water supply, and farming plots when deciding where to place the more permanent fencing.

It is very likely that your property will already have existing buildings on the land. There will probably be a house, a shed, and some other smaller structures. The benefits of rural homesteads are the flexibility to fit these existing structures into the design of your homestead and maximize the value they bring to your farm. I highly recommend that, when you start on a rural property, you renovate and update the existing structures on your farm. Refer back to the permaculture layout section so that you can establish exactly what you will need from zone 0 and 1. If you are interested in establishing or building new structures on your farm, consider the water lines and roads that you have set up. This will provide a blueprint for the best spaces to start building new structures. Also, consider what zone on your farm these spaces are in. If you have space in zone 4 to build a new building to house some tools or vehicles, it may be worthwhile to do so if there is no other room. But if you are able to build that same structure in zone 2 or 3, that will make your life easier as you are navigating your daily tasks. The last thing to consider when you are renovating or establishing new buildings on your homestead is the power needed for those buildings. There are many different options for power supplies that your homestead can have. It is probable that your property will already have access to a power grid, as that is customary for most properties, but there are other methods of energy harvesting worth considering. Water and solar panel energy are both options to consider, especially if you are building new structures on the farm.

Another crucial consideration to make when you are beginning a rural farm is the quality of your soil. The soil quality will be determined by a lot of different factors, but your best bet is to determine the soil quality on your property with a soil moisture and pH sensor. Soil can change drastically and can be enriched with some simple farming techniques. Understanding your soil quality in the building and layout stage of planning your homestead will ensure that you have time to remedy any soil issues you may face. Some strategies to try if you need to enrich your soil are to plow the soil to break up any excessively dry areas, mulch, inoculate your soil with fertilizer, or make your own compost teas.

Once you have established the layout and design of a rural farm, you will feel confident in your ability to build and maintain your homestead. The scale of permanence is a great principle to keep in the back of your head when you are planning what to buy and where to build. Keep in mind the basic necessities before you start diving into the more nuanced aspects of maintaining a homestead.

OFF-THE-GRID HOMESTEADS

Starting an off-the-grid homestead is definitely a giant leap forward if you haven't tried living off-the-grid before, but the benefits are unmatched. Living on an off-the-grid homestead generally means that you have very limited access to modern technology, electricity, and water. However, it can look different for many people. Their benefits of living the minimalist lifestyle that off-the-grid homesteading calls for is a drastic decrease in the cost of living, an opportunity to be closer with nature, and a chance to unplug from the digital world. Living off-the-grid can look like finding a rural homestead where you generate your own electricity and water with limited connection to the internet. It could also look like living in a tiny or mobile home with more freedom to travel and fewer expenses. Regardless of the style of living, the tenets for an off-the-grid homestead are that you have access to your own source of water, electricity, and resources.

All of the steps mentioned previously in urban and rural home-steading can be applied to off-the-grid living. The information that is key to learning before you start an off-the-grid homestead is how you will fully sustain yourself when your access to others may be limited. There are no hard and fast rules about how much internet access to modern technologies you can have with you while you are on an off-the-grid homestead; it will all depend on your comfort level. The key information to gather before you start is how you will get water, power, and food. Off-the-grid living is certainly not for everyone. This style of homesteading is great for people who are looking for a lower cost of living, don't rely heavily on modern technology, or who want to reconnect with nature. If you are someone who heavily relies on modern technology and the internet, this may not be the lifestyle change for you.

When you are starting an off-the-grid homestead, it is imperative that you set up a water system on your homestead that is manageable and can be consistently utilized. The tips that I gave about water storage, harvesting, and division of water become essential when you are living off-the-grid. You will want to invest a lot of time in researching the best and most cost effective strategies for water storage and harvesting well before you reach your off-the-grid homestead. Having a plotted map of the water system before you get to your farm will be essential in maintaining an off-the-grid lifestyle.

Solar panels, wind turbines, windmills, and generators are going to be your best options when exploring power sources for an off-the-grid farm. Each of these power sources come with their own cost attached, but I highly recommend that this is one of your first purchases. Having the power to heat, cool, and light your home is essential and the cost of having power is worth it. Explore all of the options for what will work best for you and the people living with you on your homestead. Similar to calculating the amount of water you will need on your homestead, power also needs to be calculated. The average modern household in the United States will consume over 10,000-kilowatt hours of electricity per year (U.S. Energy Information Administration, 2021). This is probably on the high end for someone living off-the-grid, but it is important to factor in the electricity needs of your farm as well as your home when you are living off-the-grid. There are certainly ways to maximize the power that your homestead gets. I recommend investing in high-efficiency appliances that don't require immense amounts of power so that the power you have collected, through any means, is used well.

Ensuring that you have enough food on your off-the-grid homestead will also be vital to the success of your homestead. Refer back to the hardiness and permaculture zones for what and how to plan the layout of your homestead to maximize the amount of food that you will have for yourself and your family. I will discuss the many different types of preserving food in a later chapter. For now, the essential information to gather is what your preferences are for food and how you can best accommodate those preferences on your homestead. If you are starting an off-the-grid homestead as a vegan or vegetarian, you may not need to invest in raising animals as part of your homestead and you can dedicate more space to farming and preserving. If you are starting an off-the-grid homestead with a family who doesn't have any dietary restrictions, there is an opportunity to invest time and resources into a more diverse farming layout. In either case, it is important to take stock of what you'd like to eat while on your homestead and the best ways to go about that. Keep in mind that no matter what hardiness zone you are in, there will be a season where it is much more challenging to grow crops. You will want to always grow more than you need to ensure there is food on the table every day.

BUY A PROPERTY THAT WORKS FOR YOU

At this point, you probably have an idea of what type of homestead style would work best for you. Now the question is: how do I find a property that will work for my homesteading needs? The best things to look for when you are searching for a property are where the access points are, what the local weather is, and the access to the community around you. This will vary drastically depending on the type of homestead you are looking to cultivate. For an urban homestead, this may look like searching for a house or apartment in a city that has a small backyard or basement for you to start your urban farm. For a rural or off-the-grid homestead, this will look like researching the land and laws in a specific state or province that most suits your needs.

Access to water is hugely important regardless of the type of homestead you are looking to build. Water access is highly dependent on where you are looking to buy property as each municipality has different regulations around water disbursement. There may be an option to dig a well for water on your property. Do some research for the area you are interested in buying land and the laws they have about digging wells. If you have access to a water source already on your farm from a spring or river, it is important to learn who owns that water source and how much water you are allotted. If you are in an urban area, you will likely have access to water, but the water needs for an urban homestead will likely exceed the water allotment for a residential home. Investing in alternative methods of water collection on your property will be key.

Similarly, if you are connected to a power grid, the amount of power allotted to your property will vary. Be sure to get a good estimate of the amount of power that you will have access to and what the needs of your homestead will be. It may be the case that you will not have access to excess power from the power grid and may need to invest in other creative power source options. There may also be an option to contact the local electricity company and see if you can get power lines installed on your property. This is potentially a very costly process, but it is always good to know all of your options.

For beginner homesteaders, I do not suggest getting raw land—land without any existing structures. If you are someone who is particularly skilled at building and you have the resources to allot to building new structures on your farm, go for it. But for most people, this will not be a worthwhile investment. Find a property that has an existing structure on it and work from there! It is important, if the property you are considering already has a house on it, that you get information about when the house was built. For older farmhouses, there are many expenses that will go into the renovation, maintenance, and upkeep of the building. This may be an additional headache for beginner homesteaders. It is possible to avoid this by finding a property with a newer house. If you are someone who is inspired by the old farmhouse aesthetic, buy a property with a newer home and transform it into that rustic feel. Don't go out of your way to fix up an older house if you do not have the skills to do so. It can be so incredibly costly that you won't have any income to invest in the farm.

The next step in buying a property is to budget for more than you are expecting. I highly recommend doing as much research as you can when you find a property that you are interested in, but make sure to leave a lot of cushion in your budget. If you go outside of your means, you may find that you are short on funds to develop what actually inspired you: the homestead. You're going to want to start from zones 0, 1, and 2. From a permaculture perspective, these zones will always be the most expensive because they require daily attention and maintenance. Don't bite off more than you can chew when you are in the property-planning stage and be sure to cushion the budget so that you can accomplish all the goals that you want with your homestead.

There will certainly be parts of homesteading that appeal to you more than others. Personally, I am much more interested in homesteads that are closer to the wilderness so that I can enjoy hiking and be in nature on less busy days. You may find that you are more interested in raising livestock, having a gorgeous flower garden, or living completely off-the-grid in an extreme way. All of these options are perfectly acceptable! Be sure to center your preferences and goals for your homestead when you are looking for a property. I highly recommend that you take your time when you are considering your options. This is a large investment that will take years to master. The beauty of this process is that you will feel such a great sense of fulfillment when you find a property that not only suits all of your wishes, but will also be a place you are proud of five years in the future.

There are many different laws that apply to homesteading depending on the state or providence you are in. If you want to relocate or you want to move down the road, it is important to research the laws for the area that you'd like to be in. In the United States, some of the best states for homesteaders are Idaho, Michigan, Missouri, Oregon, and Tennessee. If you are looking for a state that offers free land to homesteaders, Colorado, Iowa, Kansas, Maine, Minnesota, Missouri, Nebraska, New York, Ohio, and Texas all offer land for homesteading. States that offer the cheapest land for rural and off-the-grid homesteads are Alaska, Arizona, Arkansas, Maine, Montana, New Mexico, and Tennessee. There are certain ordinances and zoning restrictions that prohibit animals and certain farming activities. Make sure to research HomeOwners Associations (HOAs) in your area for their ordinances. Do your research on the type of zoning and ordinances for your potential property.. Don't just ask your Realtor, make sure you call the county and do the research yourself. I would hate it if you bought a property to have chickens and the bylaws state, "You can't have chickens!" There are options out there that will suit your needs. Research your area to fully understand the access and limitations that certain places provide.

4

GETTING STARTED

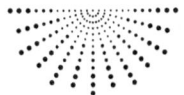

GET THE RIGHT TOOLS

*D*eciding what and where to invest money when you are starting a homestead can sometimes feel overwhelming. There are a lot of different areas of the homestead to consider and you will want to ensure that you are working as efficiently as possible. At the end of the day, we are all human and some days will feel more efficient than others. We can't always be working at peak performance, and frankly, getting away from high-stress situations is certainly why many people choose homesteading. When it comes to the best tools to have in each area of your homestead, I have broken it down into four categories: tools for the garden, tools for the shed, tools for the animals, and tools for the kitchen. In each area of your homestead, you will be performing different tasks with different frequencies. Where you plan on spending the bulk of your time is where you should invest in higher quality tools. As a reminder, be careful with your budget. You may already own some of these things and others you will have to buy, but don't go beyond your means when you are making tool-purchasing decisions. If you are finding that something will cost too much, it may be worth shifting your focus to a different area of your homestead and maximizing your gains in that area first.

Previously, I listed out the best starter set of tools for a small urban home garden. Those tools certainly apply to the tools that are necessary for gardening. In addition to the list, it is worth investing in comfortable and durable farming clothes. I suggest work jeans, comfortable cotton t-shirts, boots, overalls, or durable leggings. You may also want to grab a post and fence hole digger if you are on a larger property.

Tools for the shed are probably the most dependent category of tools that you will need for your homestead. What you choose to do with your homestead will inform what you will need to keep on hand in a shed or garage. The following is a list of all of the most essential tools to keep in your shed for a larger rural or off-the-grid homestead. For an urban homestead, the following tool list can be cut down, as you will have less need for them depending on the amount of space you have. You may find that you will need more specialized tools to complete different projects around your homestead. Use this list as the basics and add to it as you develop new ideas and projects for your farm.

- Tractor
- Lawnmower
- Generator
- Firearms for hunting
- Pocket or utility knife
- Wheelbarrow
- Reciprocating, table, circular, and/or miter saw
- Chainsaw
- Plumber's Putty
- Extension cords
- Grain mill
- Wire cutters
- Plier set

- Reusable cloths or towels
- Distilled white vinegar, baking soda, and essential oils for cleaning
- A level
- 5-gallon buckets
- Cable ties or twine
- Ratchet straps
- Tape measure
- Safety glasses
- Screwdrivers
- Drills
- Allen and socket wrenches
- Ax
- Hammer
- Shovel
- Ladders
- Duct Tape
- Flashlights and a headlamp
- Fire extinguisher

THE BASIC TOOLS THAT YOU WILL WANT TO CONSIDER INVESTING IN FOR your animals are bag balm—if you have cows or goats that you're regularly milking—feeding pans, a mobile animal crate, cattle panels, and welded wire fences. If you choose to raise animals on your farm, the type of animals that you choose will decide the tools that you will need on hand to care for them. Later, I will talk about the best beginner animals for a homestead, each having their own contingent tools that are necessary for their upkeep.

When it comes to the kitchen, your preferences will take front and center. I will discuss all of the strategies for preserving food for your family and potentially selling later. The following list encompasses the main appliances and tools that you will need to accomplish all of those strategies.

- Deep freezer
- Food processor
- Blender
- Food dehydrator
- Stand mixer
- Meat grinder
- Pressure canner
- Pressure cooker
- Hot water bath canner
- Fermenting crocks
- Vacuum sealer
- Kitchen compost pail
- Mason jars
- Cast iron cookware
- Loaf pans
- Stockpots
- Knife set
- Rolling pin
- Mortar and pestle
- Fruit peeler
- Fruit corer
- Kitchen scale
- Cutting board
- Proofing basket

PLAN, PLAN, PLAN!

After deciding what is important to you and what you want on your homestead, it is time to start brainstorming the more nuanced parts of your layout. Think long and hard about the design, because there are a lot of considerations to make. Be sure to be practical about the time it will take to build, create, or achieve the goals you are setting out, as well as the financial investment that some aspects will require. Refer back to the permaculture concepts that I mentioned earlier as the framework for how you approach designing the smaller parts of your homestead. When you have identified the type of homestead that you'd like to build—urban, rural, or off-the-grid—it is time to start trying all sorts of combinations for the layout that will work for you and your family. When you are brainstorming with a family in mind, it is important to keep a log or notebook of the ideas that you have for the homestead, draft the layout of different rooms, and calculate the resources that each area will require. If you are designing a couple of bedrooms, consider the energy needs of each area. When planning a kitchen, keep in mind the space and storage needs for each person in the family.

Plan pantry and storage space as well. During this step, account for home-canned food, dried food, cold storage or root cellar, bulk food, seed banks, oils, herbs, medicine, toiletry, batteries, candles, water, storage containers, bags, and tools. This may seem like a lot of things to consider, but when you are moving into any new property, storage is sure to become more scarce when more people are involved. On a homestead, this is even more so the case because you will need extra storage room for canning, preserving, and fermenting your harvests. It is also essential to plan space for utilities like a water heater, well pump or pressure tank, filtration system, propane tank, wood-fired boiler, wood stove, solar panels, breaker box, battery bank for off-the-grid homesteads, and/or a power inverter. Some properties will already have a home for these things that you will have to design around. Nevertheless, it is important to consider all aspects so that there are no surprises down the line.

If you are building a home, design a floor plan that uses minimal plumbing and electrical runs. This will cut down on the cost of building and digging trenches significantly. If you are not building a home, be sure to get a blueprint of the home or a thorough layout of the building so that you know where all of the pipes and electricity runs are. This can be important for maintenance and to quickly identify issues when they come up. Other areas to consider when plotting out zones 0, 1, and 2 are a garden, community-sponsored agriculture, small livestock, butchering, cheesemaking, soapmaking, woodworking, metalworking, sewing, knitting, homeschooling, home office, crafting, and/or homebrewing. Again, all of these things are contingent on what you would like to do with your homestead and how you would like to invest your time. These lists are merely options for consideration or new ideas that you might not have thought of yet.

If you are moving into a homestead, it may also be worth making considerations for accessibility. As you develop your homestead, you are going to get older. Homesteading is a long endeavor and it is important to look out for the future. As a general rule, hallways should be at least 42 inches wide, doors should be at least 36 inches wide, living spaces should primarily be on the first floor, and there should be minimal to no steps into or out of the house. Ensuring that these things are in place will not only mean that your homestead is accessible to anyone you invite over, but will also ensure that as you age, your house won't be an obstacle that you have to overcome. My last, and probably most important tip when planning, is to be flexible! Things are bound to change and that is okay. You are going to grow with the space that you have. Be creative and find solutions that will work for you and the people you live with.

DESIGN & LAYOUT

Again, when you are designing the layout of your farm, it is of the utmost importance to refer to the permaculture zones and ensure that your homestead is working for you. Designing with the permaculture and scale of permanence in mind will allow you to create a homestead that is functional, efficient, and affords you all of the things that you were looking to get from the homesteading experience. For more general tips on the design and layout of your homestead, I recommend that you start with a smaller property for your first homestead. Whether you are in a city, looking for a rural area, or living in a van, starting small will be the key to finding the successes and areas for improvement in your homesteading skills. Depending on your state, there are various ways to find cheap and affordable land to start homesteading with. It can be very overwhelming to start with a large plot of land and try to maintain it. I suggest starting with about an acre of land for your first property. There are a lot of expenses that go into starting a homestead. It is always a great practice to be thrifty and DIY as much as possible, because there are some unavoidable costs to homesteading. When you start with a smaller plot of land, you will be able to feel fully in control of the layout and design that you want for your homestead.

Setting your expectations for what will come from your first homestead is definitely a tricky process as there are many variables to keep in mind. I recommend that you focus on an easy and minimal design layout when you start so that you feel in control and can maximize your profits. For your first homestead, try to only have permaculture zones 0, 1, and 2. If you have some extra space for a zone 3, that's great, but I wouldn't recommend starting projects on zone 3 with as much fervor as the previous zones. Multiple raised gardening beds, a chicken coop, and a shed with supplies is a great starter layout for beginner homesteaders. This will allow you to feel less overwhelmed and find your homestead manageable and profitable.

The kitchen garden, or the main garden that you are going to use to feed yourself and your family, is a great thing to consider in the design and layout portion of planning. This garden is also sometimes referred to as the crisis garden, because it is pivotal to feeding the people on the homestead. The kitchen garden will always be in zone 1 on your homestead as you will need to tend to it daily. There are a couple of things to keep in mind when you are planning your kitchen garden. It is important that the kitchen garden is in zone 1, has access to enough sunlight, has proper airflow and access to water, has great soil, and is safe from anything that could damage it. The kitchen garden should be no more than a five-minute walk from the door to your house. Whether this is in your backyard or in a side yard depends on your homestead layout. You will also want to look for an area that isn't flat. Having a small slope for your kitchen garden has a myriad of benefits to the success of the garden. A small slope can help with access to the sun, irrigation, and drainage. The slope should be very slight, like a hill or ridge. If the slope is too extreme, the benefits of the sloping garden will be negated. The kitchen garden should also be placed halfway down the slope, and not at the bottom, to avoid flooding.

Sunlight, airflow, water, and soil are also vitally important to the success of your kitchen garden. As a general rule, you will want your crops to have as much access to the sun as they can get. While I mentioned earlier that each crop has specific sunlight requirements, for the kitchen garden, it is acceptable to allow as much sunlight as possible, because you will be monitoring its progress daily. If you find that a crop is getting too much sun, it is perfectly fine to re-pot the crop and move it to a slightly more shaded area. The airflow for your kitchen garden is also important. If the air around your kitchen garden is too stagnant or moist, it may cultivate fungal diseases which will destroy or greatly impair your garden. It is a little more tricky to find out how the air flows around your kitchen garden, but there are multiple online tools that can allow you to find information about the general wind speeds and their directions for your area. With some careful research, you can discover the right area for your kitchen garden to thrive. Watering your kitchen garden also takes some consideration. There may be a spring or pond above the garden that you can utilize for irrigating your crops, you may have a water tank inside your house, you can use a hose to water your crops, or you could have rainwater collection bins. In any situation, it is important that you gather the information for how much water your crops will need to thrive and the most efficient ways to water them on your homestead. There is no reason that you should be carrying gallons of water across your property every day to water your kitchen garden, so find a process that works for the layout of your homestead and make it do the work for you.

Testing your soil and understanding the viability of the soil on your homestead is the last essential tip to building your kitchen garden. There are many ways to do this, which I discussed earlier. You will want to test the soil moisture, compactness, and pH to understand how it can best be leveraged to grow your crops. Also, be sure to look out for earthworms. Worms are a good sign that the ecosystem in your soil is alive and healthy.

5
DIY PROJECTS & BLUEPRINTS

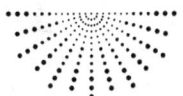

$\mathcal{N}$o matter what type of homestead you are looking to create, the sense of fulfillment you will get from building your own systems is certainly worth it. I recommend doing as much research as you can about cost-effective ways to DIY your own projects around the farm. There are so many varieties of DIY projects and outlines for you to choose from. Doing the research to find a way to build small structures on your farm will save you so much money. The following are some simple and easy DIY projects that you can accomplish on a new homestead.

GARDENING

Raised beds are a simple and easy DIY project that any beginner home-steader can conquer. A raised bed is a small garden structure where you build an enclosure for specific crops. Because the bed is raised above the compact dirt on your farm, it is easier to harvest, you have more control of the soil content, and you can even dig deeper into the existing soil for extra depth. A raised bed will save you space and also time, because a raised bed promotes fewer weeds.

Raised beds are very customizable and can be changed to fit your needs. When you are buying wood for your raised bed, I suggest that you go for cedar or redwood, depending on your budget. Both cedar and redwood are rot-resistant, however, redwood tends to be more expensive than cedar. Douglas fir and pressure-treated wood like construction pine are not ideal for raised beds, because they lack longevity and the pressure-treated wood is treated with chemicals that can leak into crops. You will want your raised beds to be anywhere from 6 inches to 12 inches deep. During the construction of your raised bed, you will need to either buy long pieces of your desired wood to cut at home or you can have them cut to size at a hardware store. Depending on the amount of raised beds that you want on your property, measure the length of each side of your desired raised beds to get the total length of the wood that you will need to buy. You will also need either 2x2s or 4x4s depending on the height and size of your raised bed. These square pieces of wood will act as support. I recommend cutting them so that they are 4 inches to 6 inches taller than the top of your raised bed and attaching them to each inside corner of the bed. These posts will support the bed as well as provide you with excess space if you'd like to tie twine or netting over the bed to protect the crops from pests. They also serve as great posts to attach a trellis for climbing plants.

Another option for a DIY gardening project is a wicking bed. A wicking bed is very similar to a raised bed, with the added benefit of self-watering. Wicking beds are great if you have a section of your garden that won't get daily attention or where there are immovable tree roots in the soil. The wicking beds can be used as a sustainable way to grow crops and also provide added access for people who may struggle to bend in order to garden.

When constructing a wicking bed, it is important to consider the size and space available on your homestead. If you have a lot of space, some people will opt to use railway sleepers for the foundation and walls of their wicking beds. Railway sleepers are the largely wooden structures that support railroad tracks. These are great for larger sections of land and, due to their thickness, they can trap moisture efficiently. For a smaller space, consider using galvanized steel. They are occasionally sold to farmers as tubs or ovals, but you can also purchase the galvanized steel sheets and shape it into an oval for your crops for a much more cost-effective project. The smallest version of a wicking bed can be placed inside a large container, so long as the container can hold all of the soil that your crops will need. Once you have established the size of your wicking bed and the material you will use to construct it, it is time to establish what goes inside the wicking bed.

Self-Watering Wicking Bed

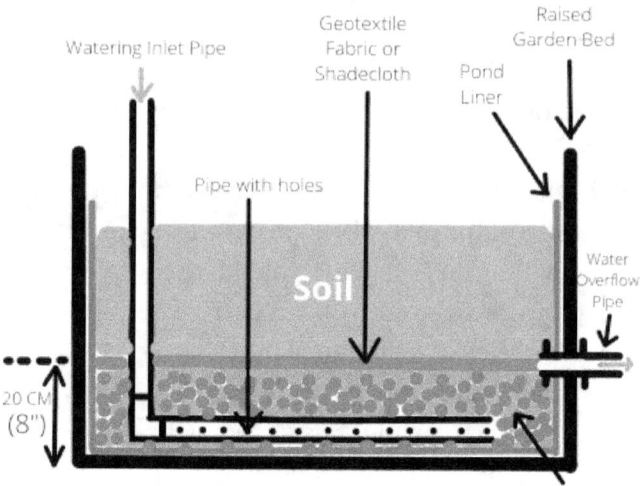

The shell of the wicking bed can be any of the previously mentioned materials. The priority is that the shell can hold all of the soil and water that your crops will need. You can find this information in previous chapters or by researching specific crops that you'd like to plant. Inside the shell, you will need to place a layer of pond liner. The pond liner can absorb large amounts of water and ensure that the wicking bed is watertight. Next, you will need to drill a hole 8 inches from the bottom of the wicking bed and fashion a pipe through it. This will ensure that if too much water is pumped through the wicking bed, it can escape. The pipe should be a threaded tank inlet or a bulkhead. You will also need an L-shaped pipe to place in your wicking bed so that water can be filtered through the bottom. The pipe can be a PVC pipe with a 90 elbow on it and will have to be long enough to reach above the soil of the wicking bed and down into the bottom of the wicking bed. Then you will want to fill the bottom of your wicking bed with porous gardening rocks. Fill the wicking bed up to the hole that you previously drilled, but be sure not to cover the pipe so that there are no blockages. Any type of porous, coarse grade lava or volcanic rock are best to use for water passage. The L-shaped pipe from earlier will need to sit about 2 inches above the bottom of the wicking basket and be covered by the porous rocks. This allows the rocks to filter the water into the soil. The second to last step is to line the layer of rocks with a shade cloth. This cloth will act as a barrier between the water and porous rocks and the soil above. You don't want the soil to seep into the rock layer because that will cause water blockages. Once you have placed the barrier, you can place your desired soil into the wicking bed. Be sure to fill the wicking bed with soil so that it falls just under the pond liner or the soil can get in between the shell and the pond liner and compromise the integrity of the wicking bed.

Both raised beds and wicking beds are perfect DIY projects for beginner homesteaders because they are relatively quick to build and will ensure that the gardening process yields quality results. There is the added benefit of water and soil control for both options and they make the back-breaking labor of gardening a little easier.

GREENHOUSE

When you start planning your layout, you are definitely going to want to consider if a greenhouse is right for you. A greenhouse is an ideal place to grow crops that would otherwise struggle outside. The added soil, moisture, and temperature control that a greenhouse can give you creates a perfect place to grow crops all year long. There are many different styles of greenhouse that range in size, cost, and effectiveness. If you are someone who is looking to build a greenhouse on a budget, the tunnel-style greenhouse is great for you. If you have a little extra room in your budget, the more traditional greenhouse build will be a great option. In either case, building your own greenhouse is certainly an option even when you are just beginning your homesteading journey. These building ideas are easy, relatively affordable, and there are countless resources you can find on how to build a greenhouse that will suit your needs.

Some things to consider before you build your first greenhouse are the location on your farm and the direction of the sun. One of the greatest benefits that a greenhouse can afford you is its ability to remain warm, but it can only do this if it is facing the right direction. Ideally, you will want to find an area on your homestead where you can place your greenhouse east to west. This will maximize the daily sun exposure that the greenhouse gets. You will also want to find a location that is in the northern part of your property. If you are building a greenhouse that utilizes a vertical gardening technique, you will want to place taller shelves on the north side of the greenhouse and shorter shelves on the south side. Another point for your consideration is the zoning requirements that you will need to meet to build your greenhouse. Regardless of the size or shape of your greenhouse, if you are establishing a new structure on your property you will need to contact your local zoning commission so that the guidelines for building the greenhouse are clear to you.

Greenhouse tunnels are an easy and affordable DIY greenhouse option for any homestead. So long as you have a plot of land to create garden rows on, a greenhouse tunnel will work perfectly for your homestead. The greenhouses are ideal for growing any crop that trellises. The shell of the greenhouse is constructed out of cattle panels and makes trellising beans, melons, tomatoes, and squash incredibly easy. To construct the greenhouse tunnel you will want 4 ½ feet wide and 16 feet long cattle panels for the shell of your greenhouse so that you can easily walk underneath them. You will also need rebar stakes that are 2 feet to 3 feet long, cedar panels cut to the length of your garden rows, and plowed garden rows. The width and length of your garden rows under the tunnel are dependent on the amount of space that you have on your farm. Once you have dug your rows, hammer a rebar stake on each end of the row and tie a string to each end. Angle the string into the row and place the cedar panels against the rows. Place stakes about 2 feet to 4 feet apart down the row and be sure to put an extra stake in place if there is a break in the cedar panels. Hammer the stakes on the outside of the string that you previously strung down the row. This will ensure that the stakes are in a straight line. Then tilt the cedar planks up so they are leaning against the stakes, facing the rows. You can use a little extra soil to ensure that the panels are standing perpendicular to the ground. Hammer the stakes so that they are flush against the cedar panels. The gardening rows should only be about 30 inches wide to ensure that you can reach across them to harvest your crops when they are ready. Leave a 30-inch lane between the two garden rows and repeat the same process on the other side of your garden rows. It is a great practice to mulch or fertilize the garden rows before placing the cattle panels. Once this is done, grab the cattle panels and bend them into place. You will want to place the ends of each cattle panel between the cedar plank and the soil. Be sure to line up the horizontal bars and have them facing the inside of the tunnel. If you leave the horizontal bars facing the outside of the tunnel, they will catch on the exterior covering. To connect all the cattle panels, zip ties will be your best friend. Starting at the top of the tunnel, zip-tie the tallest point and each side of the tunnel together. Ensure that your tunnel is completely connected and stable. If you are living in a particularly windy area, you may want to place more stakes on the inside of the tunnel to add to the structural integrity of the greenhouse. To protect your crops from wind and pests, you will need to get sheets of polyethylene plastic. The soft plastic is great for greenhouses because it will trap heat and is flexible enough that it will not tear. You can secure the plastic with more zip ties or stakes, depending on wind levels.

If you are interested in building a more traditional greenhouse, there are a couple of decisions you will need to make first. At this point, you have already established where your greenhouse will be located on your property and the amount of space that you have available to build on. The shape of your greenhouse can vary based on your preferences, but the most traditional-style greenhouses have either a dome or gothic shape. The materials that you will need for a more traditional greenhouse build are blueprints of the design that you are working with, materials for the structure of the greenhouse, polyethylene plastic for the exterior, and a ventilation system.

CHICKEN COOP

Chicken coops are also an option for beginner homesteaders as they are relatively easy and cost-effective projects if you are interested in raising chickens on your farm. Later on, I will discuss all the benefits of raising animals on your farm. There are many options to purchase a pre-built chicken coop at a relatively low cost. For new homesteaders, I think that this can be a great option. If you would like to build your own chicken coop, there are a couple of building considerations that you will first need to make. During the planning and layout phase of homesteading, the chicken coop should be placed in zone 1 or 2, depending on space. Chickens need regular maintenance and the coop should be close to your house so that you have an easy time accessing it daily. The location of your coop will also impact your chickens. You will want to find an area on your farm that doesn't get excessive amounts of sunlight. The eastern side of your house is a great area for a chicken coop. The outdoor compost bin should also be placed near the chicken coop so that you can dump any chicken waste into the bin. Chicken waste makes for excellent fertilizer for your outdoor crops.

The best starting chicken coop to build yourself is called Harriet's House by Karl Caden. This coop style allows for up to 5 chickens with 2 nest boxes. The coop is raised off of the ground to discourage predators from getting into the

chicken coop. There is also a fenced area for the chickens to graze with a small door for you to transport the chickens for selective grazing. It is important to regularly allow your chickens to selectively graze to reduce the risk of parasites and improve their food options. The overall dimensions of a Harriet's House base are 3 feet by 12 feet, and the coop is 2 ½ feet by 3 feet. The materials that you will need to build the coop are cedar or redwood slabs that are cut to the dimensions of the build, heavy-duty hinges and latches to prevent predators from accessing the coop, a power drill, and wire mesh for the outdoor pen. I would recommend against using plywood for the build, as some plywood is pressure treated and the chemicals in the plywood can be dangerous for the chickens. However, for the exterior roof of the chicken coop, plywood is perfectly acceptable.

Another option for a DIY coop is to construct a chicken coop that leans against the east side of your house. This style of coop is less time-consuming to create and the design is relatively simple. This coop calls for a hatch at the top to remove any eggs, clean, and feed the chickens, as well as a hatch on the side of the coop to allow the chickens to graze. It becomes a little tricky with this style of coop build to clean the coop out as there are only two access points into the coop, but since the side hatch can be resized to nearly the entire length of the coop for easier cleaning, and due to the simplicity of the build, it is worth the effort. The overall dimensions of this style of the coop are 8 feet by 1 ¾ feet. This coop is smaller than Harriet's House and can hold up to 3 chickens. The building materials are virtually the same as Harriet's House, but the construction of this coop will take less time and materials.

Whichever style of coop you choose to either purchase or build, having a chicken coop on your first homestead is definitely one of the most manageable and profitable aspects of a first homestead. There are a lot of potential options that you can have from raising chickens and the benefits that the chickens themselves bring to the farm are worth it. In building a chicken coop on your first homestead, you will also need to build a pen for your chickens as it will greatly improve your homestead. In the Harriet's House build, there is a small pen built into the construction. For the simplified chicken coop, there is no pen associated with it and you will need a dedicated area for your chickens to graze. There is commercial-grade poultry netting that is a perfect investment for constructing a chicken pen. You will also want to invest in T-posts, poultry net staples, a staple gun or hammer, a post digger, and either a sledgehammer or post driver. Once you have established the area and size of your chicken pen, plot the spots that you will add the posts to and dig the posts 6-8 inches into the ground. Cut the poultry netting to the size of your pen and secure the netting to the T-posts with the poultry netting staples. Chicken waste is a great fertilizer, allowing your chickens to selectively graze can improve their diets and decrease the risk of wildfires, and chickens and their eggs can become supplemental income for your homestead.

COMPOST BIN

At this point, I have referenced both a kitchen compost bin and an outdoor compost bin for your homestead. Compost bins can provide endless benefits to your homestead because the composted material is a great way to maintain a sustainable homestead, fertilize your crops, and reduce your carbon footprint. Your compost bin should be a collection of plant clippings, plant pruning, food scraps, and any other organic material that you collect on your homestead. As a general rule, your compost bin should not be excessively smelly. So long as you ensure to regularly moisten and add organic green matter that is nitrogen-rich to your compost bin, it should be relatively smell less.

The most cost-effective compost bin for a beginner homesteader is to recycle an old plastic container with a lid that fits tightly. Fill the container with soil from your homestead and drill holes into the top. I suggest adding foliage as well as the soil so that there is enough nitrogen-based plant material in your compost bin. Add scraps to your compost bin, ensuring that you regularly stir and moisten the contents of the compost bin. If you have a small kitchen compost bin in your kitchen, be sure to regularly dump the contents of that bin into the larger bin. The plastic container compost bin should have a home outside that is not directly in the sun. It should take two to three months for your compost to be ready to use on your farm. If you set up multiple of these bins in the fall and sustain them throughout the winter, you will have plenty of DIY fertilizer to use on your crops during the growing season in the spring.

Another method for building an outdoor compost bin is to use pallet wood. However, there are some serious dangers associated with wood pallets. If you are reclaiming the pallets, it is likely that you don't know where they are coming from. Depending on the purpose that the wood pallets served, they may have been exposed to harmful chemicals and you don't want those chemicals on your homestead. There are two ways that wood pallets are treated as decided by the USDA. They can either be heat-treated, which is safe for your homestead, or they are treated with chemicals, which are not safe for your homestead. Each pallet should have a stamp on them to indicate if they were heated or chemically treated. If you see an "HT" stamp, the pallet is heat treated and safe to use. Similarly, if you see a "DB," "KD," or "EPAL" stamp on the pallets, they are safe to use. These stamps stand for debarked, kiln-dried, and European Pallet Association, which no longer chemically treat the wood. Alternatively, if you see a "EUR" stamp or the pallets are colored, they were chemically treated and should not be brought onto your homestead.

Once you are sure that you have secured safe wood pallets, the construction of a pallet compost bin can start. To make a wood pallet compost bin you will need three pallets, a piece of plywood, wood screws, a screwdriver, gloves, and a shovel. To construct the compost bin, you will secure the pallets together so that they are standing at their tallest when placed vertically. Create an open square with the pallets and then secure a 3 foot piece of plywood to the base on the opened side. This opening will allow you to place compost bits into the bin, shovel the contents, and water the compost bin. The wood pallet compost bin is a much more fixed structure on the farm and you should ensure that you find a place on your homestead that doesn't get direct sunlight. The added benefit of the wood pallet compost bin is that you have the opportunity to compost more scraps and yield more fertilizer for the growing season.

6
GET READY TO GROW!

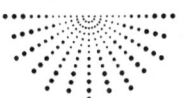

PLANTING YOUR FIRST GARDEN

*P*lanting your first garden on your first homestead is certainly an exciting feat. At this point, you have put in hours of work and preparation to determine exactly where and what you want your homestead to be. Planting the first garden is a milestone in your homesteading journey. I have discussed some strategies for what to grow depending on where you are, where to place your gardens, and strategies for getting the most success from your crops. There are a couple of other aspects to planting your first garden, such as a no-dig garden as well as testing the pH in your soil.

A no-dig garden, sometimes called lasagna gardening, is the practice of layering different types of soils and fertilizers on top of each other to fill a gardening bed. The purpose of no-dig gardening is to create a thriving composting plot that will deliver essential nutrients to your crops. There are many different layers that go into a no-dig garden, and all of them are materials that you can easily find around your homestead. One strategy for no-dig gardening is to use a raised bed and layer in newspaper, lucerne or alfalfa, compost, straw, compost, and straw. Between each layer of the no-dig garden, you will want to water the contents. Once all of the layers have been placed and watered, dig a hole in the top layer, fill it with compost, and plant your desired seeds. This type of layered design creates a carbon-rich environment for your crops to thrive in. Another strategy, if you want to forego the raised bed, is to start a no-dig garden on the ground. This strategy requires a little more preparation before you can start layering materials. If you are layering your no dig garden on top of the soil, you don't need to prep the area. If you are starting on concrete, you will need to add a layer of dried sticks and leaves that are at least 4 inches thick. If you are starting on grass, be sure to sprinkle the grass with organic fertilizer and water first.

All of these styles of no-dig gardening require preparation before your first season of gardening on your homestead. At the start of the spring or autumn season, in order to maintain your no-dig garden, you will need to add a layer of mulch or manure to the top of your no-dig garden, and then a layer of straw. Be sure to water the layers and dig the same holes to fill with compost before you begin planting for the upcoming season.

Testing the soil pH is essential to planting your first garden. Before you start planting, it is a great practice to test the pH of your soil to determine how acidic or alkaline it is. Most soil moisture readers will also be able to tell you the pH of your soil. Alternatively, there are soil pH testing kits that you can purchase. Each crop that you plant will have a preferred pH range; determining the pH of the general area will best help you either choose which crops to plant or point you toward a method to alter the pH. Having the desired pH in your soil will allow your crops to take in more nutrients and determine the balance of healthy bacteria and fungus in the soil. Depending on where your homestead is, the pH in your soil will vary widely. As a general rule, you will want the pH of your soil to be between 5.5 and 7.5. Again, each crop will have a desired pH. If you are finding that the pH in your soil is not where you'd like it to be, there are a couple of methods to use to change the pH of your soil. For acidic soils, you will want to apply organic fertilizers, compost, or mulch to your soil and till it regularly. For alkaline or base soils, you will want to add sulfur as well as organic fertilizer to your soil. Alkaline soils will take more time to change their pH levels as it is harder to naturally add minerals to soil to bring down the pH level. Composting and finding the right balance of organic fertilizers will be your best bet.

The best crops to grow, dependent on their pH levels, span through all hardiness zones and are great for beginner gardens. For slightly acidic soils (4.5-6), eggplant, potatoes, rhubarb, and sweet potatoes will thrive in a kitchen garden. Fruit trees, blueberries, blackberries, and raspberries will thrive in slightly more acidic soil. For soil with a pH level between 6-6.5, beans, brussel sprouts, carrots, kale, radish, squash, and tomatoes will grow beautifully. Apples, cherry, peach, and pear trees will also thrive in this pH range. For slightly more alkaline soils (6.5-7.5), arugula, asparagus, beets, broccoli, cabbage, lettuce, and okra will grow well. Fig and plum trees will also do well. All of this is to say that you are going to want to determine the pH of the soil on your homestead, adjust your fertilizing strategy to accommodate for the pH level, and determine which crops will do the best with certain pH levels.

Beginner Vegetables

For newer farmers, I recommend starting your seeds inside rather than outside. Starting your seeds inside allows you to get a head start on the growing season, especially if you are living in a colder climate area. The best vegetables to start inside are vegetables that don't have deep roots. Deeply rooted plants don't like to be moved during the growing season and you may risk killing or injuring the crop by moving it outdoors. The easiest starter vegetables are lettuce, green beans, radishes, tomatoes, zucchini, peppers, pumpkins, beets, carrots, cucumbers, chard, spinach, kale, and peas. If you are able to grow these specific crops will depend on the hardiness zone that you are in and the access that these crops need to warm weather. Lettuce, tomatoes, peppers, chard, spinach, kale, and peas can all be started indoors. Green beans, radishes, zucchini, pumpkins, beets, carrots, and cucumbers need to be started outdoors. Choosing the vegetables for your first garden should depend on what you like to eat, how much you eat, what is available to you locally, and how much time you are able to commit to maintaining your first garden.

In order to start seeds inside, you will need quality seeds, a grow light, clean containers, potting soil, and water. Each seed will have information about how long it will need to mature, this will inform you on how early you should start sowing your seedlings before the start of the growing season. A great practice is to place your seedling containers in either a greenhouse or place a transparent container over the seedlings so that they retain their moisture. You will need to water your seedlings often. It is perfectly fine to remove them from their containers to check that the roots are moist before watering. Feel free to get thrifty with how you pot your seedlings. You can certainly invest in seed trays or plug trays, but reusing plastic food containers or egg cartons is perfectly acceptable.

Now that your seedlings are growing, it is time to start planning your outdoor garden. To plan your garden, *The Old Farmer's Almanac* has online tools available for you to plot the size and quantity of crops that you'd like to plant in your garden. The online tool is able to tell you the best ways to rotate your crops in the following season, allow you to plan for future seasons, and send email updates on new tools and farming techniques. For beginner farmers, this tool is essential to understand every aspect of your gardens. After you have a plan for where your garden will be and how big your garden is, consider the wind, drainage, and soil nutrients. I have previously discussed all of the ways to monitor these things. Double-check that you have every aspect necessary to have a successful garden in place.

When your seedlings are ready to be transported to your outdoor garden, there are a couple of steps that you will need to take to ensure a successful transfer. A week or two before you transfer the plants outdoors, take the seedlings outdoors for a couple of hours and leave them in a shaded spot that doesn't get much wind. Extend this period of time a little each day as your crops begin to get accustomed to being outdoors. Be sure that the plants have enough moisture while they are outside so they don't get too dry and begin transpiration—when plants release water vapor as a result of changing temperatures. Once the weather conditions are right for your crops and you've allowed them to grow accustomed to being outdoors, you can transport them into your garden.

Pest Protection & Plant Health

Pest protection and prevention is one of the most tricky skills for a new farmer because there are so many variables that will bring pests into your garden. Insects, deer, and rodents can all make a home in your garden if there is no protection for your crops. There are countless strategies out there to prevent pests from getting into your garden but many of them rely on pesticides and chemically-based cocktails that may damage your crops or lead to potential adverse health outcomes for you and your family. The following are organic and sustainable strategies to protect your crops from unwanted visitors.

To best prevent insect damage to your crops, you will want to discourage them from showing up in the first place. The best way to do this is to remove any weak plants, rotate crops between seasons, cultivate healthy and organic soil, water early in the morning, practice no-dig gardening techniques, and use seaweed in your compost.

If you have run into a pest problem in your garden, be sure to disinfect all of your tools after handling the infected plants. In more extreme gardening practices, a great way to avoid pests is to encourage garden snakes to take up residence in your garden. Garden snakes eat pests and will keep your garden healthier and happier. There are also various insects that will keep your garden free of pests. You can encourage these insects to thrive near your garden by planting a nearby flower garden. Hover-flies, lacewings, ladybugs, nematodes, and praying mantises are all great insects to allow residence around your garden as they will naturally decrease the risk of garden-damaging insects. In the case that your garden has too many insects for your liking, be sure to avoid using store-bought sprays that kill insects as they can kill the beneficial insects as well. Depending on the crops and the type of insects that are feeding on them, there are many different types of natural sprays that you can create to discourage these insects from feeding on your crops. A quart of water, ivory soap, and some canola oil in a spray bottle will smother the insects that you don't want in your garden and won't risk any damage to your crops.

In more rural settings, there is a chance that your farm and gardens may be visited by deer. Deer love to snack on leafy greens and foliage. It can certainly be a task to encourage them to stay away from your crops, but due to the number of greens that one deer can eat in a day, it is certainly worth the effort. One strategy that you can try is to mix milk, eggs, water, detergent, and cooking oil into a spray bottle and spray down your crops. This mixture tastes bitter to deer and it will encourage them to look elsewhere for snacks. It will also remain on the crops in between rain days because the egg has an adhesive quality. Another option to encourage deer to stay away from your crops is to tie a bar of soap to a string and hang it in the middle of a bush or crop area that the deer have been targeting. The smell is too strong for them and they won't venture near. Similarly, if you fill a small cloth bag with hair from your hairbrush, the deer will recognize that the smell is human and not come near. You will need to be sure that you check on these deer repellents regularly so that they are still in place. The deer will certainly return if one of these repellent options is not maintained.

For small rodents, it is incredibly important to secure your compost bin. Rodents will love the extra snacks that they can find in your compost bin. I recommend getting a tight lid or welded metal netting and heavy-duty latches to secure your compost bin. A great organic way to repel all rodents is to get a cloth or cotton balls and soak them in peppermint oil. Leave the cloth or cotton balls in a relatively dry area so the peppermint smell doesn't get diluted by the rain, and all the rodents will stay away.

These pest prevention strategies are great for your plant health as well. After all, if your crops aren't being targeted by insects, deer, and rodents, they will live healthier lives. Another option for maintaining your plant's health is to regularly prune your crops. Pruning is the process of selectively trimming your crops, bushes, and trees to ensure that they have healthy and strong branches. The key things to look out for when you are pruning are decaying or dead branches, diseased leaves and wood, crossing branches, and any unwanted roots or weeds. Seasonally, there are better times to prune than others. As a general rule, it is great to prune shrubs, fruits trees, and evergreens from February through April. The more delicate flowers, flowering shrubs, and fruit trees should be pruned in May and June. Your crops should be pruned of any unwanted, damaged, or diseased shoots in June and July. Limit the pruning of any crop or tree in August through December because it could stimulate more growth that will ultimately go unharvested as you move into the colder months.

Companion Planting

When you are planning which crops to grow in a growing season, it is important to consider companion planting. Companion planting is the practice of simultaneously growing crops that support each other and create all sorts of benefits for your farm. Companion planting deters pests, attracts beneficial insects, improves plant health, suppresses weeds, improves soil quality, and larger plants act as shade for smaller plants. It is completely possible to research all of the crops that you want to plant in a season and discover what their companion crops are. Some general guidelines on what companion crops are best to grow next to each other, or in the same raised bed, are:

- Tomatoes can be grown alongside cabbage, basil, parsley, and borage.
- Cucumbers go well with corn, beans, peas, beets, celery, lettuce, and dill.
- Borage is a companion crop to strawberries.
- Carrots will thrive when planted with sage.
- Garlic and cabbage are companion crops.
- Sunflowers, cucumbers, and green beans can also be planted next to each other.
- Mint should always be planted nearby as it provides a lot of natural insect repellent, but it has an aggressive growth cycle that could overtake other crops.

If you are looking to leverage companion planting in your garden, *The Old Farmer's Almanac* website has a comprehensive list of every starter vegetable and the best companion crops to grow with it. It is a worthwhile practice to research which crops will support others when you are deciding what to plant in each growing season.

7

KEEP IT FRESH

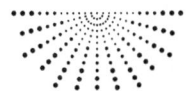

*N*ow that you have an understanding of what to plant, where to plant it, and the best ways to leverage your permaculture layout to yield the best results, it is time to determine how you are going to store your harvests and keep them fresh. The main reasons that food spoils when you store it are because there are microorganisms causing problems, enzymes that ripen the harvests, air, light, pests, physical damage, temperature, and time that all impact the freshness of your food. When your harvests are exposed to too much air, light, or varying temperatures, the oxidation promotes a chemical process that will change the color, nutrients, and taste of your food. Physical damage and leaving your food unattended for too much time will also promote microorganism development.

In order to keep your harvests fresher for longer, you will want to store your food in either cupboards, refrigerators, or freezers that are all less than 60 °F to avoid microorganism development. The USDA recommended temperatures for cupboards and pantries are 50-70 °F, 34-40 °F for refrigerators, and 0°F for freezers. Investing in airtight containers and bags will also prevent pests and physical damage to your food.

Some examples of crop harvests that need special attention are apples and pears, cabbage, leafy greens, mangoes, onions, potatoes, and squash. Apples and pears, and other pitted fruits, should be refrigerated in plastic bags and preferably in produce drawers. Unripe fruits can be left at room temperature with good airflow, but once they start to ripen they need to head into the refrigerator. Cabbage, and similar crops like broccoli and cauliflower, should be refrigerated in sealed containers or bags. You can refrigerate them whole or chopped. Leafy greens of any variety should be refrigerated before they are washed. When you are ready to eat them, wash and chop them. Washing the leafy greens before you are ready to prepare them for a meal can add excess moisture that will spoil the greens. Mangoes can also be left out at room temperature if they are unripe, but once the mangoes ripen, place them in the refrigerator separate from other fruits. All onion and garlic varieties should be stored in a dark and cool place that doesn't have high humidity. It may be tempting to throw them in a root cellar, but onions and potatoes shouldn't be stored in the same containers. Keep them separated for extended freshness. Lastly, squash, zucchini, and pumpkins can be kept at room temperature with good airflow, but should not be stored with unripe fruit.

PRESERVING YOUR HARVEST

To extend the value and uses of your harvests even further, you may want to consider preserving your food. There are many different preservation options that you can utilize to keep your food delicious and long-lasting. Canning, pickling, dehydrating, freezing, curing, and smoking are only a few options. Alternatively, you could try root cellaring, sealing, fermenting, and jamming. All of these practices take time commitment and initial investment in the materials needed to preserve in specific ways. Keeping your harvests fresh and ensuring that they last you through the winter season is a great way to cut down on food costs. Preserving is essential if you are considering an off-the-grid homestead, but for each style of homesteading, it is worth considering the benefits of preserving your harvests. The preserving practice can also translate into another source of revenue for your farm.

Canning & Pickling

Canning and pickling your harvests is a great option if you want to maintain the fresh flavors from your crops. There are a couple of considerations to make if you choose to can or pickle your crops. The canning and pickling process requires a certain set of kitchen appliances that are essential to the practice. If you can or pickle your crops incorrectly, they can quickly spoil or cause health complications from contaminated food.

Canning is the practice of heating jars that are filled with chopped vegetables or fruits and sealing the jars. This process destroys any harmful microorganisms and preserves the fresh flavors from your chosen fruit or vegetable. To safely practice canning at home, there are three different methods that you could try: atmospheric steam canning, boiling water baths, and pressure canning. Before you decide on a method of canning, it is important to ensure that you have safe jars and lids at your disposal. It is the safest to buy new jars, but if you are recycling used jars, check that the jars and lids are devoid of any cracks, as this will compromise the canning process. Once you have determined which jars and lids you are going to use, you will need to decide on the recipes and methods for packing the jars. The recipes that you use are completely up to your preferences and there are a myriad of recipes available to you online. To pack your jars, you can either use a hot or raw pack method. The hot pack method calls for boiling the food that you are going to place in the jars and packing the food and some of the boiling water into the jar. Be sure that your jars aren't cold before you do this or you will risk cracking the jar. The shrinkage that takes place when hot packing will allow you to add extra water so that the food has a little extra room. The raw packing method calls for chopping raw food and placing it in a jar. You will then add boiling water and citric acid or syrup to the jar and make sure that you have enough space between the top of the water and the lid. Either option is perfectly acceptable, however, the hot pack method will preserve more of the color of the food that you are placing in the jar.

Atmospheric steam canning is best for any crop that is naturally acidic with a pH of less than 4.5. You should absolutely not use this method for vegetables or any crop that has a pH of more than 4.6. To practice atmospheric steam canning, you will need a steam canner that requires you to place your jars in a rack and allow a water reservoir below to steam the cans. This process is called *thermal treatment* and will seal and prevent any harmful organisms from developing inside the jars. The atmospheric steam canning method is a faster and more energy-efficient option for your kitchen. The boiling water bath method for canning your harvests is a safe method for fruits, jams, and jellies. Similar to atmospheric steam canning, you will not want to use this method for any vegetables or crops that have a pH of more than 4.6, as this may result in botulism. To practice the boiling water bath method, your jarred food needs to be saturated in citric acid and placed in boiling water. Once the jars are fully submerged in boiling water, they will be sealed and safe for storage. The last method is pressure canning. Pressure canning is a safe method for canning vegetables or crops that have a higher pH. It is also possible to pressure can meats, seafood, and poultry. A pressure canner can be purchased at any kitchen appliance store. The pressure canner will require that you place your jars in a couple of inches of water, seal the pressure canner, and allow it to reach the set temperature to ensure that your canned goods are safe for consumption and storage.

After you have stored the canned goods for a period of time, it is important to check them for spoiling. To check if your canned goods have spoiled, do not eat them, instead check that the lips are intact and not bulging. If you open the can and see that there is off-color food, leaking, mold, or an odor, immediately dispose of the can. For low acid canned foods, it is possible that the botulinum toxin has been produced and the disposal process needs to be more thorough. Follow your state or province guidelines for how to best dispose of the cans. For high acid canned foods, the content of the cans needs to be disposed of and the cans need to be detoxified. Again, each state and province has their own guidelines on how to best do this.

Pickling is also a great option for preserving your harvests. Pickling is the process of preserving foods in a brine solution and allowing the food to ferment. It is important to consider headspace when you are pickling. Headspace is the room between the top of the food or liquid in a jar and the lid. This space allows for the fermentation process to happen and release gas. Each pickling recipe will call for different amounts of headspace depending on the ingredients. There are two methods for pickling at home: boiling water baths and quick pickling. The boiling water bath method is identical to the boiling water bath method for canning food. The same storage and food safety precautions should be followed for pickling as well. The quick pickling method is a fast process that calls for placing your chopped fruits, vegetables, or herbs into the brine and refrigerating the jar. The benefits of the quick pickling method are that the pickled food can last in the refrigerator for up to four months and the short pickling process means that you will have pickled foods ready within a couple of days.

There are many options for pickling different fruits, vegetables, and herbs that you grow in your garden. Pay attention to each recipe, as it will call for different headspace, brine solutions, and pickling times. The storage process for canning and pickling is the same if you use a longer pickling process and the same botulism risks arise with pickling as well. Be careful if you are engaging in canning or pickling your harvests; while it can be a worthwhile experience and a great way to keep your produce tasting fresh, there are safety procedures that are pivotal to adhere to.

Dehydrating

Dehydrating your harvests is a great method for preserving food as the process is easy and has been done for tens of thousands of years. There are many different types of dehydrating, but a common method that you will see in modern kitchens is the electric dehydrator. These machines mimic the process of naturally dehydrating food with one quick and easy appliance. However, for more natural approaches, you can air, sun, oven, or microwave dry your harvests. The benefit of dehydrating your harvests is that you can dehydrate fruits, vegetables, herbs, nuts, meats, and seafood. For the best dehydration results, you will want to pick fruits and vegetables right when it becomes ripe, use fresh and lean fish and meat, soak nuts and seeds overnight in water, and harvest herbs in the mornings and before their flowers bloom.

Aside from investing in a dehydrator, some other tools that you will need before you can start dehydrating your harvests are a paring knife, a handheld fruit and vegetable peeler, a food processor, and a grater. These tools will make the dehydrating process go a lot faster and ensure that your produce is cut and cored before you eat it. If you are interested in preserving the color of your dehydrated produce, you can add citric acid, fruit juices, and ascorbic acid to your produce. Citric acid will give your fruits and vegetables a slightly tart taste, but it will retain its color. Fruit juices can be used on fruits and vegetables if the produce is submerged in the juice for up to 10 minutes. Ascorbic acid is the most effective at retaining the color of your produce during dehydration. Adding your sliced produce to ascorbic acid for up to an hour, rinsing, and then dehydrating will retain nearly all of the original color.

When you are ready to start the dehydrating process, consider these different methods. Air drying your produce calls for laying your harvests on a baking sheet in a dry and shaded area. The best produce to air dry are leafy greens and herbs, because they are more delicate. You will want to keep your produce out of direct sunlight as the intense heat can damage the produce and leave you with dried greens and herbs that are wilted and discolored. Sun-drying calls for placing your produce on baking sheets or racks and placing them in direct sunlight. This works great for sliced fruits, because the sun will dry the natural water that the fruits contain efficiently. The process of sun-drying will take several days, so it is important to place a transparent or mesh screen over the fruit to prevent pests from getting to it. The ideal temperature for sun-drying fruit is anywhere with a minimum temperature of 85 °F. The humidity will also impact the sun drying process; you want to have a humidity of around 60% to yield the best results. Oven-drying produce is a very similar process to using a dehydrator. To practice oven-drying, you will want to set your oven to its lowest temperature (usually 140 °F or less) and place your produce on baking sheets. This method works great for any type of produce, but you will need to remember to keep the oven door open so that excess moisture can escape. Each type of produce that you place in the oven to oven-dry will require different amounts of time in the oven to dehydrate. Microwave dehydration can be a great option if you are not looking to invest in another kitchen appliance, however, microwave dehydrating only works for fruits and herbs. Place your sliced fruits and herbs on a microwave-safe plate and set the microwave to its defrost setting. This process should take up to 40 minutes for fruits, and up to 3 minutes for herbs, depending on the wattage of your microwave.

Freezing

Freezing your harvests is by far the quickest and easiest way to preserve your food and retain all of the original flavors. If you have a freezer in your kitchen or a large freezer in your shed, utilizing these spaces to preserve your harvests will save you time and effort, and deliver great-tasting food. Keep in mind that the only way that freezer-preserved produce loses its flavor is if it is not stored properly. Produce that comes in contact with the air in the freezer will begin oxidizing and completely lose its taste.

When you are considering freezing your harvests, be sure that you keep the freezer at 0 °F and avoid fluctuating the temperature. Large fluctuations in temperature can cause the produce to defrost and refreeze, and this process contributes to freezer burnt food. Use airtight containers and vacuum-sealed bags when you are freezing meat and seafood. If you are buying new containers for storage, look for labels that say moisture-resistant, durable, and leak-proof. You also want to avoid buying containers that are too rigid and will crack in the freezer. Be sure that you cool your foods to room temperature before placing them in the freezer.

Curing & Smoking

Curing and smoking your meats, if you are raising animals on your farm, is a great way to preserve the flavor and taste of the meat. Before you start curing or smoking, it is important to make sure that you have sanitized your work surfaces or you have disinfectant available to you when you want to begin the curing and smoking process.

During the portioning step of curing and smoking various meats, be sure to sanitize your work surface in between different meats to avoid cross-contamination. When you are storing meats before curing or smoking them, raw products should be separated from cooked products during storage. No raw meat products should be stored at temperatures higher than 40 °F as there is an increased chance of microorganism growth.

Curing any animal meat is a great way to preserve your food. The curing process calls for adding salt to your raw meat to draw out any excess moisture and kill any unwanted microbes. Curing meat should never be done to salvage the meat; you should only cure fresh meat. An optional step that you may consider before curing your meats is to age them. If you decide that you want to age your meat, you must keep the raw meat in a refrigerator below 40 °F. When you remove the raw meat from the refrigerator, be sure to allow it to thaw at an even rate. If the meat thaws too quickly, it can cause it to spoil. To cure the meat, you need to add a healthy serving of salt and thoroughly coat the entire piece of meat. Only use food-grade salt without any additives. You may also opt to use curing mixtures or compounds. There are many safe and quality curing mixtures that you can make at home or buy locally. If there is nitrate in your curing mixture, it is only safe to use for dry-curing. If there is nitrite in your curing mixture, it is safe to be cooked, smoked, or canned.

Before curing the meat, it is essential to allow the meat to thaw completely while refrigerated if it was previously frozen. Only after the meat is thawed can you add the curing mixtures (either homemade or store-bought). Ensure that the curing mixture is thoroughly and evenly applied to the meat. Cure the meat between 35 °F and 40 °F. Don't use the same curing mixture for different meats. You can separate the mixture into containers before you start the curing process so that there is no risk of cross-contamination. Any cut of meat that is less than 7 oz should be cured in a refrigerator for up to 7 days.

Smoking your farm animal meats is another method of preservation that is great for the beginner homesteader. Smoking meat is the process of exposing meats to heat and smoke for long periods of time. This process is almost identical to barbequing meat. Smoking raw meat dehydrates the produce and kills any microorganisms that could cause you harm. When you are smoking different meats, it is important to have an internal temperature reader on hand because different types of meats need to be at different internal temperatures to cook all the way through. You can store cured or smoked poultry for up to 2 weeks in the refrigerator, or 1 year in the freezer. You can store fish for up to 2 weeks in the refrigerator or 3 months in the freezer, and you can store meat in a vacuum-sealed bag at 40 °F in the fridge for up to 2 weeks. It is not advisable to store meat in the freezer for beginners after smoking because there are increased risks of spoilage and contamination.

STORAGE

It is clear that storage of your preserved harvests will take up some space on your homestead. Depending on the method that you use to preserve foods, some have more space requirements than others. Refer back to the permaculture design and the scale of permanence principle when you are planning out the space for storage that you will need. Keep in mind where on your property you are able to build a survival storage system, the shelving that you will need for the space, and any temperature requirements that the food you are storing has. In addition to storage that you will need for preservation, it is worth considering the space that you will need for survival storage. There are always unpredictable events that will take place from power outages, snowstorms, and natural disasters. It is important to think about storing non-perishable items on your homestead in the case of an emergency. The best beginner storage items to keep on hand are rice, beans, pasta, salt, pepper, and other non-perishables and herbs that you enjoy. The importance is that all the food you store will not spoil in storage.

Some of the best foods to keep in your survival storage are non-perishable items that you can get from your local grocery store, canned and pickled goods that you've made at home, and any of your favorite snacks that will last a while when stored. Utilize the preservation methods above especially if you are living in an area where access to food may be limited. If you are living in a place where you are less concerned about food shortages, start with a survival storage system that will last you and your family about three days. It may be the case that you will need more than this, but starting small when you begin living on your homestead will make this process much more manageable.

Another consideration worth making is the caloric requirements for yourself and the people you live with. When you are planning your survival storage system, keep in mind how many calories each person will need and be sure that you have enough food stocked up. You will not need excessive amounts of food to do this, but it is important to consider. If you are in a situation where you are not able to leave your house, ensuring that everyone is getting the calories that they need to function will be a great way to keep everyone happy and productive. If everyone is not able to get the calories that they need, you will see your family become lethargic and irritable.

8
SO YOU WANT A COW?

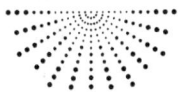

*R*aising animals on your farm can be an incredibly fulfilling and lucrative endeavor. If you are living on a homestead with your family, animals can be a great addition that will bring happiness and life to your farm. Bear in mind that when you are planning the design of your farm, there will likely be some space that animals can occupy. You don't have to commit to buying and raising animals on your homestead right away, but it is definitely worth leaving a little room in your designs if you think that you may want some down the line. The following are some examples of the best starter animals that you may want to raise on your farm. Each animal needs specific water, food, space, and attention to yield the best results. If you feel like you are ready for the time and energy commitment that comes with raising animals, here are some ideas to keep in mind:

BEST STARTER ANIMALS

Chickens

 Chickens are a great starter animal because they don't require much space, their needs are easy to meet, and they can produce an additional source of revenue. Each chicken that you have in your coop will require four square feet of space. There are a lot of designs available for very intricate chicken coops. I previously listed two types of chicken coops that are relatively simple projects. There is always the option of buying a chicken coop outright. The important thing to keep in mind is that chickens require protection from predators, a contained space to move around, a nesting box, and a place to roost. So long as your coop meets all of these requirements, there is no need to overdo it. Avoid chemical washes to disinfect the coop; there are plenty of homemade solutions that will disinfect the coop without compromising the health of your chickens. A solution of water, soap, and white vinegar will take care of most of your disinfectant needs.

You can raise chickens for eggs, meat, and breeding. Investing in dual-purpose chickens—chickens that are raised for their eggs and their meat—is a great practice for a beginner farmer because you may have extra chickens that are either too small for meat or aren't laying eggs. Dual-purpose chickens are also hardier and will be more forgiving animals to raise for your first homestead. The best dual-purpose chicken breeds are Araucanas, Barred Rocks, New Hampshire Reds, and Rhode Island Reds. When you are raising chickens, they will need access to water, organic food, and room to graze and roam. For new farmers, I suggest buying chicks or mature chickens. It is a very delicate and time-consuming process to incubate chicken eggs and it's far more prudent to spend your time learning about chicken health for live chickens. You can purchase chicks locally or order them online.

Once you have your chickens, allow them to be free-range when you can. Chickens need exercise and space to roam around in order to keep them healthy and stress-free, but be sure to keep them out of your garden because they will uproot your crops. You will also need to feed your chickens. Chicken feeders and waterers are simple construction projects that any beginner can complete and you will save money by making them on your farm with the resources that you've already collected. A great practice is to feed your chickens crushed eggshells to improve their calcium. Optionally, you can give your chickens the kitchen scraps that you've collected in your kitchen compost bin. These kitchen scraps are a cost effective and nutrient-rich snack. If you are living in a colder climate, it is a worthwhile investment to get a heated water bowl for your chickens. Regular water bowls can freeze over and you'll spend pointless time breaking the ice and refilling the bowl. Purchasing a heated water bowl will make your life easier and your chickens will have clean water all day long. Chickens are relatively low-maintenance animals, especially if you have other animals on your farm that require more attention. Establishing a routine for when you refill their feeders, water, and check the coop for eggs, is a great way to ensure that your chickens are getting the attention that they need. Along with the routine that you have established for your chickens, it is also important to regularly clean out and refill the chicken coop with hay and bedding. This will keep your chickens healthy and make sure that your eggs stay clean.

Rabbits

Rabbits are another great animal to have on your first farm. They are adorable and will bring a smile to your face as you tend to them. You can raise rabbits for their meat, fur, and to sell as pets. Depending on your rabbit breed, they will prefer different types of food. As a general rule, rabbits eat hay and leafy greens. Plotting an extra area in your garden for leafy greens that are specifically for your rabbits is a great practice. When you are planning the layout of your farm, you will have to decide if you want a hutch setup or a colony setup. Hutches are great if you are raising rabbits for their meat and fur. Hutches are small coops that are elevated from the ground and house a couple of rabbits. You will want to separate your female and male rabbits into different hutches to avoid a bunch of baby rabbits. The best rabbit breeds to have, if you want to sell their meat, are New Zealand White, California rabbits, Florida Whites, and Standard Rex rabbits. A colony setup is great if you are raising rabbits to sell as pets. A colony setup calls for a larger coop, resembling a chicken coop, where all of your rabbits live together. In either case, don't isolate any single rabbit, because they are social creatures and this will lead to increased stress and potential health issues. Rabbits are prey animals and you will need to make sure that there is plenty of protection all around their enclosure so that no predators can get in. You will also need to protect your rabbits from the elements. During the summer months, be sure their enclosure is shaded, and in the winter months, be sure that their enclosure is kept dry to avoid ice build-up.

Whether you have rabbit hutches or a colony setup, it is incredibly important to regularly clean your rabbits' homes. Cleaning their homes will drastically reduce the risk of them contracting coccidiosis, a common bacterial illness in rabbits.  Use organic soap, white vinegar, and water to clean out the rabbit enclosures. If you have hutches for your rabbits, it is common that the rabbits will be standing on wire racks when they are in the hutches. Be sure that you allow your rabbits to have space to roam and rest their feet. You can set up a modular pen on patches of grass to allow your rabbits to get some needed exercise as well. Be sure to look out for predators during their exercise time and take the necessary precautions. Alternatively, you can place a fleece blanket or soft wood in their hutch for them to perch on. Regardless of your rabbit enclosure setup, there will be times when your rabbits will need to nest. Typically this happens before a female rabbit is about to give birth. If your rabbits require a nesting box, it is important to change the hay out of the nesting box daily to ensure that there isn't any rabbit waste.

Rabbits have sensitive ears that are prone to ear mites. Rabbits with ear mites will have scabs and excess ear wax. A preventative measure to ensure that your rabbits don't develop ear mites is to regularly clean your rabbit's ears with cotton swabs filled with either olive or vegetable oil. Do not use essential oils on your rabbit's ears, as it can be toxic for them. Depending on your rabbit breed, you may need to invest in pet nail trimmers. Some rabbit breeds need their nails regularly maintained and this will ensure that they don't hurt any other rabbit or themselves.

Ducks

Ducks are another adorable farm animal that are relatively easy to raise on your first property. Ducks, like chickens, need four square feet of indoor space per duck and ten square feet of space outdoors. Similar to chickens, ducks will need a safe and dry place with plenty of bedding and hay at night. You can raise ducks for the meat and eggs. The best duck breeds for their meat are American Pekin ducks, the best duck breeds for eggs are Indian ducks, and Appleyard ducks are great for both. Not all duck breeds can fly so when you are considering the coop for your ducks, make sure you have protection in all directions if you have flying breeds.

If you are raising ducklings, they will need to be kept warm, protected from predators, and have access to water for brooding. Brooding is when ducklings are getting comfortable with swimming. They are incredibly clumsy and messy when they are young, and there are many DIY options for homestead brooding ponds if you are raising ducklings. Add some stones into their brooding ponds so that the ducklings don't get stuck on their backs and drown.

When you are feeding your ducklings, they can eat non-medicated chicken feed. There are options for waterfowl feed that you can buy from a pet store, but waterfowl feed is a little rarer than chicken feed. When you are buying food for ducklings, it is important to also grab niacin to put in their food. This is a vitamin that is central to a duck's health that isn't found in chicken feed. Niacin will support a healthy growth cycle for your ducklings. Mature ducks can drink up to one gallon of water per day, so it is important to keep a plentiful water source for your ducks to drink from.

Bees

Keeping bees on your farm has the dual purpose of generating revenue from honey and keeping all of your flower gardens well-pollinated and thriving. While I understand that bees aren't for everyone, they are certainly very good little helpers for your first farm. All private beekeeping will need to be registered with your state or province. Before you invest in a colony of bees, you will need to get the proper equipment. You will need a hive, hive tools, smoker, and protective clothing. There are many options for beehives that you can get prior to purchasing bees. A popular option is the Langstroth Hive. A hive tool looks like a crowbar and is used to separate the lid of the hive from the frame when it becomes sticky. A smoker allows you to calm your bees if you need to move their home, inspect the hive, or remove the honey. Before buying your bees, it is important to invest in all of the protective clothing for handling bees. These include a hat with a veil, jacket, and gloves.

Bees can travel up to three miles away from their hive to collect pollen and nectar, however, if they have to travel too far from their hive, they will be too tired when they make it back to the hive and the colony will not be as productive. A great practice is to keep a large flower garden near your beehives to encourage honey production. There are many breeds of bees that are worth considering based on how much honey production you would like and the maintenance that you can commit to for your bees. The most popular bee types in the United States are Carniolan honey bees, Caucasian honey bees, German Black honey bees, Italian honey bees, and Russian honey bees.

You will need to check your beehives at least once a week to check for any health issues with your bees or potential predators. The most common bee predators are bears, birds, skunks, possums, mice, other bees, and insects. Bear prevention is no small feat, but if you live in an area with a large bear population you will probably already have electric fences in place to protect your homestead. These fences are even more important if you have beehives. If you have beehives, don't hang any bird feeders on your farm to attract more birds, as they will target the hives. Elevate your beehives to prevent small rodents like skunks, mice, and possums from getting to the hives. You can also place cones with the narrow end up around the legs of the hives to discourage climbing. Other bees, wasps, and yellow jackets will target beehives that are weak. To prevent these attacks, the best thing you can do is ensure that your colonies are thriving.

To collect the honey from your beehives, you will need to use a hive tool to extract the panels from your hive. Once you've taken out the panels, you can slice the combs of honey from them and transport them into your kitchen. To properly harvest your honey, you will need a heated uncapping knife, uncapping tank, and a honey extractor. All of these tools will ensure that you are getting delicious and pure honey from your beehives. Joining a community of beekeepers is a great way to get started if you are interested in beekeeping. Beekeepers communities can lend you valuable information about the best practices for keeping bees in your area. In a digital age, this is easier than ever and the information that you can get from these communities will make your first beekeeping experience fruitful and enjoyable.

Goats

There are dairy goats, meat goats, fiber goats, and pet goats to choose from when you are considering goats on your farm. Dairy goats are great if you want to produce goat milk and cheese on your farm. Each dairy goat breed has slightly different tasting milk and it is important to consider your preferences when selecting a goat breed. The best dairy goat breeds for beginners are Alpine, Nigerian Dwarf, Nubian, LaMancha, Saanen, and Toggenburg goats. Raising goats for their meat is certainly an option as well. The best goat breeds to raise for their meat are Kiko and Boer goats. You can also raise goats for their fleece. Fiber goat breeds that are manageable and make lovely fiber are Angora, Cashmere, and Pygora goats. There are also goats that you can raise on your farm for pets. These pet goats can either be for your own enjoyment or they can be an additional revenue stream. Pygmy goats are a popular favorite for pet goats because they are friendly and intelligent.

You will need to build a home for your goats. A classic-style barn or coop is great for goats but they will need much more room than chicken, ducks, or rabbits. Goats also need room to walk around. Consider building a fenced area that your goats can graze and exercise in. Goats also love to climb; placing something in the middle of their enclosure to climb on will be a great way to entertain your goats. Otherwise, they will find ways to escape. The fencing around your goat enclosure needs to be relatively sturdy or the goats will find a way out. Welded wire fencing or electric fences are great options. An easy way to feed your goats, if you have wire fencing around their enclosure, is to attach feeding buckets that are easy for your goats to access. Goats will also need lots of water that you change daily. If you live in a place that gets cold, you may want to invest in a heated water bowl for your goats. Maintaining the hay in your goat's home is also very important. Goats need clean hay, and any moldy hay needs to be removed immediately or it can risk the health of your animals. A balanced diet for a goat consists of pasture grazing, hay, grain, healthy minerals, and baking soda. The dietary needs of your goats will depend on their breed and the purpose you have for raising goats. Be sure to research the exact needs of the goats that you want to have on your farm. If you are raising goats for their milk, it is important to invest in some initial equipment to make the milking process easier. A milking stand that is at least one foot off the ground will make milking a lot simpler. Optionally, you can add a small feeding basket to the end of the milking stand so that your goats are occupied during milking.

Pigs

Pigs definitely come with a lot of stigmas, but if you raise pigs on your farm with care, they will live happy lives that are very profitable. A great practice for raising pigs is to raise them from infancy to slaughter. Be sure to buy multiple pigs if you can, because they are social creatures and will develop physical and mental illnesses if isolated. Some pig breeds that are manageable are Berkshire, Hampshire, Kune Kune, Large Black, and Pot Belly pigs. Each breed has preferred living conditions that you will need to keep in mind. When you are considering the space that you will need for your pigs, it is very similar to the amount of space goats need. Pigs like to roam, graze, and forage, but they are not very tall. A one to two foot welded wire gate around your pig enclosure will keep them in. They will also need a large coop to protect them from the weather. A pig's diet consists of pasture grazing, hay, produce, grain, protein, grubs and earthworms, and pig-safe snacks. Pigs drink a lot of water and will need a lot of access to clean drinking water.

Some other benefits of raising pigs are that they are very smart. Pigs can easily be trained and are very entertaining to have on your farm. However, pigs will start to destroy your farm if you leave them unattended and they get bored. They are very smart and will find ways to entertain themselves if they are not attended to. Pigs also have a reputation for being smelly. If you regularly wash your pigs and keep their enclosure clean, they will not smell at all.

Cattle

If you are starting your first homestead, cattle are a tricky first animal to raise. I suggest starting with some of the previously mentioned animals before diving into the world of cattle raising. If you are not on a very large property, it is not advisable to raise cattle. Cattle need a lot of space to roam, graze, and exercise. Without a lot of land, your cattle will experience high amounts of stress that can lead to drastic health complications. For a new farmer, it is better to wait before considering if you want to raise cattle on your land.

However, if you feel confident that you'd like to raise cattle, they can be great for meat, milk, and hides. Depending on the breed of cattle that you are interested in raising, they will have temperature preferences. Some dairy cattle are not suited for warmer climates because they will produce less milk. The stress from the heat can also leave you with irritable cattle. The best climates to raise cattle are moderate climates that range from 40 °F to 75 °F. Cattle want to be housed in dry and shady climates to reduce heat stress that they may experience outside. Cattle, more than any other animal that I have mentioned, need access to a lot of clean drinking water. It is also important to test your drinking water. It has been shown that cattle that drink water with high sulfate and chloride content can have adverse health outcomes.

9

SHOW ME THE MONEY!

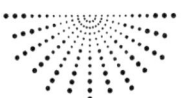

*B*eing out in nature is not only a great practice for finding calm and beautiful moments, it can also be an incredibly profitable experience. When you are considering what type of homestead you want, the design and layout of the farm, and the ways to accommodate your family, it is also time to think about how you can make your homestead work for you. There are many different areas of your farm that can be a source of revenue. The following are some ideas to get you going, but I implore you to use your creativity to discover a profitable way to homestead. It will feel even more rewarding to turn your farm into a business and share all of the incredible things that you have achieved with the outside world. If you can find the intersection between a passion you have and a homemade way to create it, share it with others, because they will certainly value it.

PROFITABLE HOMESTEADING

There are three areas on your homestead that can prove to be profitable: the garden, the farm, and your workshop. The garden encompasses your crops, orchard, and creative ways for your community to invest in your harvests. The farm is all of your animals and the products that your animals can make. Last, the workshop is all of the areas on your property that you can leverage to make homemade crafts, start entrepreneurial endeavors, and package up all of the products that your farm produces.

From the Garden

When you are considering leveraging your garden to turn a profit on your farm, it is important to separate your kitchen garden from a larger garden. Your kitchen garden is specifically for your use and a way to sustain yourself while you are maintaining your property. The larger garden can be used for all sorts of creative enterprises. Seasonally, it is a great idea to utilize your larger garden to provide things that people are buying in bulk. During the earlier seasons, it is a great idea to plant roses in your greenhouse and sell them for Valentine's Day. Later in the year, you can plant a pumpkin patch or corn stalks that will be a hot commodity during the fall. You can also invest in some pine saplings and create a pine orchard for the holiday season.

If you are more interested in growing a wide variety of crops and using the companion planting strategy, a great way to engage with the community and make money is to participate in farmer's markets. While farmer's markets are mostly seasonal, there is an opportunity to sell your fresh produce as well as baked, canned, dehydrated, and pickled goods. There is also a high value placed on dried herbs and spice mixes that are easy to harvest, dry, and sell at farmer's markets. Don't forget to also visit your fruit tree orchard before the farmer's market to sell fresh fruits as well.

If you are finding that the time investment for getting all of this produce ready in your first year is overwhelming, you can also sell seeds and seedlings from your garden to other farmers or home gardeners. Seed cultivation will naturally occur as you harvest crops from your garden and greenhouse. Storing these seeds takes a couple of additional steps, but they are definitely manageable. Alternatively, you can propagate seedlings and sell them. Propagation only takes about a week, depending on the seeds, and many home gardeners love buying seedlings because there is a much higher success rate for planting seedlings than germinating seeds.

The last option for making your gardens profitable is to start a Community Supported Agriculture operation (CSA). A CSA is the process of selling shares of your harvests to people who support your farm. This requires you to sell produce that you harvest on your farm. Additionally, investors receive scheduled bundles of produce from your farm. This is a great way to receive consistent income for your farm and engage with the local community. Not every state and province allows for CSAs, but some do. Research if this is an option for you and definitely take advantage of the opportunity.

From the Farm

Animal products are another great source of income. Chicken eggs, duck eggs, and milk are all readily available to you if you raise animals on your farm. You can also process some of the animal products and sell cheese, butter, and fiber or fleece. Artisan goods that are created on a farm are highly valuable in a society that is moving away from highly processed foods with lots of additives. The market for authentically sourced goods is out there.

While slightly more time consuming, honey, sausage, jerky, and hides are another option. Cultivating honey in your first year on the farm requires some initial investment, but at the end of the warmer seasons, a thriving bee colony can create pounds of honey that you can process, package, and sell right from your kitchen. Processing meats from your farm animals is a great source of income. There are also options to partner with your local vendors to sell the meats for you.

If you are not interested in killing your animals to turn a profit, you can also raise farm animals to sell. Chickens, ducks, rabbits, and Pygmy goats are all popular pets. There are many families that are looking to buy pets, and these cute and fluffy creatures certainly fit the bill. With internet connection and a couple of posts, you are sure to have buyers lined up for your adorable, humanely-raised farm animals.

From the Workshop

Items that you can make inside your home, in a craft room, or in the shed, are endless. Consider what brings you joy and where you like to spend your time. If you are someone who enjoys knitting or sewing, you can turn the goat fiber that you've collected into yarn. Maybe you enjoy carpentry or metal work? Utilize your shed and the wood that you've cultivated from your coppice garden to create stunning handmade pieces of furniture. There are so many options to choose from that you will surely find something you enjoy and make it profitable for your farm. Other handcrafted items that you can make on your farm are soaps, lotions, mason jar baking kits, beeswax candles and lip balms, ceramics, and clothing.

Another lucrative and incredibly fulfilling way to make money on your farm is to set up a small brewing operation. You are sure to have excess fruits from your orchard that you can turn into cider, beer, mead, or wine. Canning and bottling the homemade brews can definitely become more costly, but there are opportunities to partner with brewing companies or local markets and let them handle the canning and bottling process.

If you are not a crafty person and would rather spend more time on your farm than anywhere else, there are opportunities to sell lumber, firewood, straw, and hay bales. These resources will be readily available all over your farm and you can package them up and send them on their way cheaply.

In a digital world, there are also a lot of options to choose from once you feel like you have a handle on your farm. You can start a blog, an online class, write a homesteaders cookbook, or start an informational YouTube channel. All of these avenues have the potential for monetization that will supplement your income. Photography and videography can also be a creative outlet that will bring in income. You will likely be living in a very beautiful place, and leveraging the photos and videos that you take of your farm on stock image websites is a great way to make some extra cash.

If you have some extra room on your farm, you may also consider creating a space that you can list on Airbnb. Many people love to escape from their busy lives into nature, and your farm would be the perfect place. This is also a relatively passive income stream that only needs to be managed in-between guest visits. Your local community can also be a great way to make money and stay connected with the people around you. There are many restaurants that are interested in serving farm-to-table meals that would gladly purchase your farm produce. Alternatively, you could host your own farm-to-table dinners that community members would pay for.

GET INVOLVED IN THE COMMUNITY

It is very likely that you will have a local community wherever you choose to start your first homestead. A great way to stay connected with your community is to partner with local vendors, organizations, and community outreach programs. Depending on your comfort level, there are many different community organizations that would either buy produce from your farm, want to visit your farm, or ask you to consult on new and developing projects. Staying connected with a group of people will not only mean new connections and networking opportunities, but the ability to immerse yourself in groups of like-minded individuals.

Going to conferences is another great way to get helpful tips and feedback from farmers who were or are in the same place as you. There are thousands of farming, homesteading, and off-the-grid living conferences in North America every year. Many of them have even gone digital so that you can participate in them without leaving the comforts of your home. Getting involved in your community may also mean attending social events that are specific to your interests. There are groups for beekeepers, homesteaders, animal raisers, and much more. These groups are an excellent excuse to meet new people, feel connected to a larger community, and discover new skills that will make your homesteading experience richer.

If you are a particularly tech-savvy person or you are living in an isolated area, there are also many online communities that you can join. There are online groups on Facebook, Discord, and many other platforms where you can share helpful tips, meet new people, and discover new strategies. You may even find a new passion or an idea for a project you hadn't considered before. If you can't find a group of people that share a particular interest that you have, start your own group! There are bound to be people who are interested in the same things that you are that would benefit from a new community.

The last, and most crucial step, to getting involved in a community, is to stay in touch. Whether you met online or in person, remember to reach out to those people that you got along with. Send thank you messages or reminder texts to the people that you want to keep around. While we are all so interconnected, that interconnectedness is negated when we don't make an effort to reach out to others.

10

CUT THE TIES

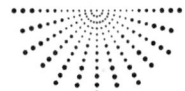

I mentioned earlier that off-the-grid homesteading is certainly an option when you are considering which type of experience you want to have. I definitely have a bias when it comes to off-the-grid living because I have been practicing wilderness survival for over ten years. I absolutely love the outdoors and being disconnected from modern life. However, there are some pros and cons to living off-the-grid that I think are valuable to mention.

Some of the benefits of going completely off-the-grid are that it is incredibly cost-effective, you have the flexibility to live anywhere you want, it is a sustainable and eco-friendly practice, and you are living a self-sustaining lifestyle. Off-the-grid living is cost-effective because you forego the modern costs of a house, rent or a mortgage, and many other costs of living that come from living in urban areas. The flexibility to live wherever you want and move when you want to is also a huge benefit to living off-the-grid. This is especially beneficial if you are living in a tiny home, van, or mobile home. Practicing off-the-grid living is also a great way to be sustainable and eco-friendly. When you are off-the-grid you have to get really creative with how you dispose of garbage and where you get supplies and resources. There are also psychological benefits to living off-the-grid. You become entirely self-sufficient when you live off-the-grid and the reliance that you have on your own choices is a great way to develop a rich sense of self and autonomy.

I would be amiss if I didn't mention the cons of living off-the-grid. These include the initial costs of setting up an off-the-grid lifestyle, the initial setup and maintenance, and the limited power supply. When you are living off-the-grid, you need to establish quickly where you are getting water and power from. There are options for how you can do this, but each option does present an initial cost. Similarly, all of those systems that you put in place need to be maintained, and this will require you to research, learn about the systems, and learn the best way to take care of them. This process can be time-consuming and labor intensive. There will also be limited access to power depending on where you choose to set up your off-the-grid farm. Power will be your best friend, but often, when you are off-the-grid, the set up and maintenance of the power doesn't end up being cheaper than living in an urban center.

The flexibility to live wherever you want with off-the-grid lifestyles is truly a wonderful thing because it brings immense amounts of freedom to your life. If you are interested in starting an off-the-grid farm or lifestyle, but you are on a tight budget, consider researching if your state or province has free land programs. In the United States, Iowa, Kansas, Nebraska, and New York all offer free land programs that are worth considering if you want to live off-the-grid in any of these places. Each state that offers free land has a couple of requirements that need to be met before you can move in. I encourage you to research where you want to live and creative solutions to obtaining a plot of land that will work for your needs. Iowa offers free plots of land in Manilla and Marne. Both towns are suburban areas with very low costs of living. Kansas offers plots in Lincoln, Marquette, and Mankato that are also in suburban areas. If you are looking for more of a wilderness experience, Iowa and Kansas may not be for you. Nebraska offers free plots in Curtis and Elwood. Both of these towns are much more rural and great for starting a farm. If you are considering an urban homestead, Buffalo, New York has a thriving urban homesteading program that brings urban renewal to the city.

GETTING THE NECESSITIES

Water

Living off-the-grid means that the basic necessities you are used to become things that you need to establish and truly consider. One of those necessities is water. At this point, you have probably identified that you want to live off-the-grid, where you want to live, and what type of homesteading experience you are looking to have. A crucial consideration that you will need to make is where you are getting water from. I mentioned earlier that it is far more cost-effective to leverage the existing natural water structures on your farm for water. It is a great practice to set up a water tank or pump in an existing water source, filter the water, and use it for all of your watering needs. However, there are two other options for getting water that cost a little more but will inevitably make your life easier.

The first option is to dig a well. Constructing a well on your property can cost several thousand dollars, because it is a new structure on the farm that will require special equipment to build. If you have the resources to invest in building a well, and you have weighed the benefits of doing so, go for it. The first thing you will need to know is the topography of your land and the quality of the groundwater. This information can be found relatively quickly online. You will also need to know if there are any septic tanks or leach fields under your property. When you are constructing the well, you will absolutely destroy any progress you are making if you hit one of these lines. I highly encourage you to contract someone to build the well on your property and leave the potentially dangerous parts of building a well to a professional.

If you are looking for a more budget-friendly option for getting groundwater on your farm, you can install a water pump. Installing a water pump will require you to do the same research as you would for a well, invest in some speciality equipment, and get digging. The tools that you will need to install a water pump are a wellpoint, well pump, post hole digger, sledge hammer, pipe wrenches, rise pipes, pipe coupling, sive cap, and thread compound. All of these materials can be purchased at a hardware store. To begin installing the water pump, you will need to determine the correct spot and the correct wellpoint for the ground in your area. There are different wellpoints made of different materials depending on the density and composition of the ground. Then you will want to dig a whole that is 3 feet deep and slightly larger than your wellpoint. Lubricate the wellpoint and place it in the hole. Attach the rise pipe and secure the wellpoint to the ground. Attach another rise pipe and stop when you hit an aquifer. Add the water pump to the top of the structure and pump out water. Be sure to test the quality of your water before you start drinking it to ensure that it is safe.

There are old tales about the best way to determine where to place a well on your farm, such as water witching, water dowsing, or divination. If you are spiritually-minded, this process may appeal to you. These methods call for holding either a two-pronged branch or tool and walking along your land with the tool facing the ground. You will know when you have reached a good spot for your well or water pump because the tool will pull down towards the ground. This is certainly not an exact science, but you will find many stories of people touting how well it works over the course of history.

Electricity

Off-the-grid electricity is certainly a necessity that you will need to consider when you move away from urban areas. It is true that off-the-grid power can be more expensive than living on the grid, but most of the expenses for electricity come from the upfront costs and the cost of battery banks. There are five types of energy generation that you could invest in when you are living off-the-grid: a generator, geothermal energy, micro-hydro energy, solar energy, and wind energy. Generators are the least sustainable option, but they are a great Plan B if your primary system goes down. Geothermal energy is the practice of leveraging the heat from the ground to power your home. Micro-hydro requires that you are near flowing water—the energy of the flowing water is converted into power for your home. Solar energy relies on the sun, so you will need to be in an area that gets consistent sunlight to generate power through solar panels. The last option is wind energy. This method requires you to invest in a windmill or turbine to generate power which needs to be stored in battery banks.

The other upfront cost that is pretty steep when living off-the-grid is the cost of batteries. Battery banks are a great way to store the power that you have collected through whichever method that you prefer. The benefit of battery banks is that you can connect them to any appliance or fixture on your farm that requires power to run. Additionally, if you have a generator, your battery bank can fuel your generator to light your home, leave your refrigerator and freezer running, and provide central heating and cooling. In any situation that you find yourself in, be sure to do a lot of research on the best options for the area that you want to live in and that will suit your lifestyle. It may not be a smart investment to get a generator if you are living in a van or mobile home because you won't have the space for it. If you are living in a permanent structure, you can leverage multiple types of energy sources that will keep a large scale farm running smoothly.

OFF-THE-GRID FOR THE WHOLE FAMILY

Going off-the-grid with a family is no small feat, but it is possible! In the same way that the solutions to obstacles that come up on your farm will require creative solutions, the same can be said for living off-the-grid with your family. Some additional considerations that you will need to make is how you will work from home and home-school younger children. In most states of the United States, children are required to go to school until they are 18 years old. If you are choosing to homeschool your kids, you will also need to be working from home so that you can best support them and your homestead. Clearly, the working-from-home option has become a lot more accessible due to the Covid-19 pandemic and accessibility through the internet. Going off-the-grid with your whole family will necessitate that you have water, electricity, internet, and sustained power. Consider all of these aspects closely before you begin your off-the-grid journey so that you can truly reap all the benefits and your family can do the same.

Homeschooling

Homeschooling your young ones is a great option if you want to keep the whole family connected through nature. The benefits of being in nature will also extend to your kids. However, it is crucial that your children are getting the education that they deserve while on your off-the-grid farm. There are benefits and drawbacks to homeschooling that I am sure you've encountered before. The benefits to homeschooling your children is that there is more freedom and flexibility in their schedules, receiving an individualized education, and specialized homeschooling options. The drawbacks of homeschooling your children are additional work and time-commitment for the whole family, a decrease in opportunities for social interaction, and a large stigma around homeschooling. The important thing to remember when weighing the pros and cons of homeschooling your children is your reason for starting an off-the-grid lifestyle. These lifestyles are certainly not for everyone, but if you believe that living off-the-grid would suit you and your family well, there are tremendous benefits and you can make it work for everyone involved.

When you homeschool your children, there is an increased sense of freedom and flexibility. When kids are in a traditional school setting, there are often relatively strict guidelines around where they should be, how they should behave, and the unspoken social cues that they need to follow—all of which are normal for socialization. When you homeschool your kids, they will be able to take breaks when they need to, put a difficult topic down and return to it when they are ready, or have a snack when they are hungry. This is also great when paired with the individualized education that your child will receive from homeschooling. With this option, kids are able to get extra help in areas that they struggle with and can be accelerated in areas that they are thriving in. I also highly recommend homeschooling for children who are neurodivergent or who have learning disabilities. This method is great for them, because they get the individualized learning that they need to be successful. It is also worth considering the specialized homeschooling options that are available to you and your family. While you can certainly take on the task of learning all of the things that your child needs to know and teaching it to them, there are many online resources for homeschooling that are available to you. I think it is a great idea to enroll your student in an online homeschooling program because it will track their progress, individualize their learning, and allow you access to view their successes and room for improvement. Homeschooling can be incredibly stressful for parents who feel the need to also become a teacher in every subject. There are options so that you can continue doing what you love around your farm while monitoring the progress of your student.

The drawbacks of homeschooling your child are the work and time-commitments that it will require from everyone in the family. This is a difficult obstacle to overcome because you want your child to succeed in school, but you will also have to balance all of the homestead tasks and any unforeseen circumstances that come up. It will feel frustrating if you need to take a day off from being your child's homeschooling teacher to handle that and watch them struggle on their own. I suggested earlier, for this exact reason, that you enroll your student in an online homeschooling program. However, if you want to homeschool your child on your own, I highly recommend that you find a pre-written curriculum to work with. EngageNY is an incredible resource for all homeschooling students because it has an English and Math curriculum for all students. The other drawback of homeschooling is the lack of social interaction that your child will get with their peers. This can be a tricky thing to navigate because there is a scientific basis for the benefit that children get from being around their peers. What I suggest is allowing your kids to participate in programs or groups with their peers locally. I previously talked about all the ways that you can make money on your farm and a lot of those ideas involve engaging in your local community. Bring your children with you and allow them to have the needed social interactions that they will crave. The last obstacle to tackle with homeschooling is the stigma. I have no hard and fast rules about how to overcome the stigma that children will face as a result of being homeschooled. The best thing that I can offer is that you let your child know that the only opinion of them that matters is their own. Teaching your child valuable skills about self-worth and authenticity will be their best tool in overcoming any stigma that comes their way.

When you are considering where you want your off-the-grid

homestead to be, there are a few states that will make homeschooling your children easier. Alaska, Connecticut, Idaho, Illinois, Iowa, Michigan, Missouri, New Jersey, Ohio, and Oklahoma all have no-to-low regulations on homeschooling children. These states are great because the process of letting the state know that you are home-schooling your child is quick and easy. The state will have very little interference while your child is being homeschooled. States that have very high regulations for homeschooling are Massachusetts, New York, Pennsylvania, Rhode Island, and Vermont. These states require you to perform many tasks in order to ensure that your child is getting the best education that they can. While their mission is noble, this may be an obstacle that you can avoid by not living in these states.

Working from Home

Working from home has become a much more accessible practice as a result of the Covid-19 pandemic. I highly encourage you to find a way to work remotely if you are interested in off-the-grid living. This becomes extremely important if you are living with your family, as you will need to attend to them, your farm, and your job. It is far easier if you can do all of these things from one location. I mentioned earlier all of the ways that you can make money on your homestead; you can truly turn any of those ideas into full-time jobs that will support your family and your farm.

If you have other skills that you want to leverage to make working from home easier, you can certainly do so. On every online job posting website, there are options to work remotely. You don't have to use your farm as a money-making operation. Whatever your case may be, working from home when you are living off-the-grid will make your life easier and you will be able to enjoy all of the reasons why you chose to live off-the-grid in the first place.

Leave a 1-Click Review!

Customer reviews

★★★★★ 5 out of 5

3 global ratings

5 star		100%
4 star		0%
3 star		0%
2 star		0%
1 star		0%

⌄ How are ratings calculated?

Review this product

Share your thoughts with other customers

Write a customer review

AFTERWORD

At this point, you have all of the beginner tools that you will need to conquer homesteading. Go out there and use them! Consider where you want to be in the world and the opportunities for farm development in those places. The USDA hardiness zones will help you understand the potential harvests that your farm can have when you discover where you want to live. Once you have decided where you want to live, consider what style of homesteading you want to practice. I talked about urban, rural, and off-the-grid, but you may decide on some combination of these. Don't be afraid to take leaps of faith or come up with creative solutions. This journey is about meeting your needs and fulfilling a desire to be closer to nature.

Don't forget to leverage the permaculture zones and scale of permanence when you are developing the design and layout of your property. These principles cannot be overstated, and they will make all of the difference for the longevity of your farm. I also want to encourage you to build new structures and systems on your farm. If you aren't someone who is comfortable with manual labor or you are inexperienced with it, take a class, watch a video, or consult a professional. In every way possible, you want to be in control of your property and your access to nature. Building your own systems and structures on your farms will aid in feeling in control. There is also the added benefit of feeling a sense of accomplishment when you complete a task. You can build anything from a chicken coop, to a well, to a solar power grid. The options are endless and I highly encourage you to take action into your own hands.

The cost of homesteading is no small consideration. When you are planning and designing your property, consider the initial costs and the returns you can make on your investment. Raising animals, starting a community-sponsored farm, or working from home are all valuable considerations to make when you are in the planning stage. Also, remember that there are so many different ways to make money on your farm. There are creative solutions to be found in every corner of your homestead that you can leverage to make your farm profitable.

The last piece of advice that I want to leave you with is that you are not alone. There are thousands of people who have chosen to live a homesteading lifestyle. The communities that can help you are out there. It is up to you to reach out to them for the help and support that you need. Join online groups, go to conferences, and remain in touch with the people that you connect with. Homesteading can sometimes feel like an isolating process, but it doesn't have to be. You are in control and this journey is about how you can best connect with nature to feel like the most authentic version of yourself. I have also created an online community for beginning homesteaders. Join our Facebook group, Northeast Homestead Gardeners and Foragers, for more tips, updates on upcoming books, as well as the ability to interact with hundreds of other homesteaders just like you. Join our community here: https://www.facebook.com/groups/northeasthome stead.

Now go out there and get gardening, building, milking, composting, harvesting, and thriving! Do not put this book down and not take action. The biggest tip I can give to beginners is to take the first step and do something! This is your life and we only have a finite time on this beautiful earth; make sure to make the most of it. I wish you tremendous success in your homesteading journey. Talk to you soon.

SURVIVAL HANDBOOK OF MEDICINE AND MEDICAL EMERGENCIES

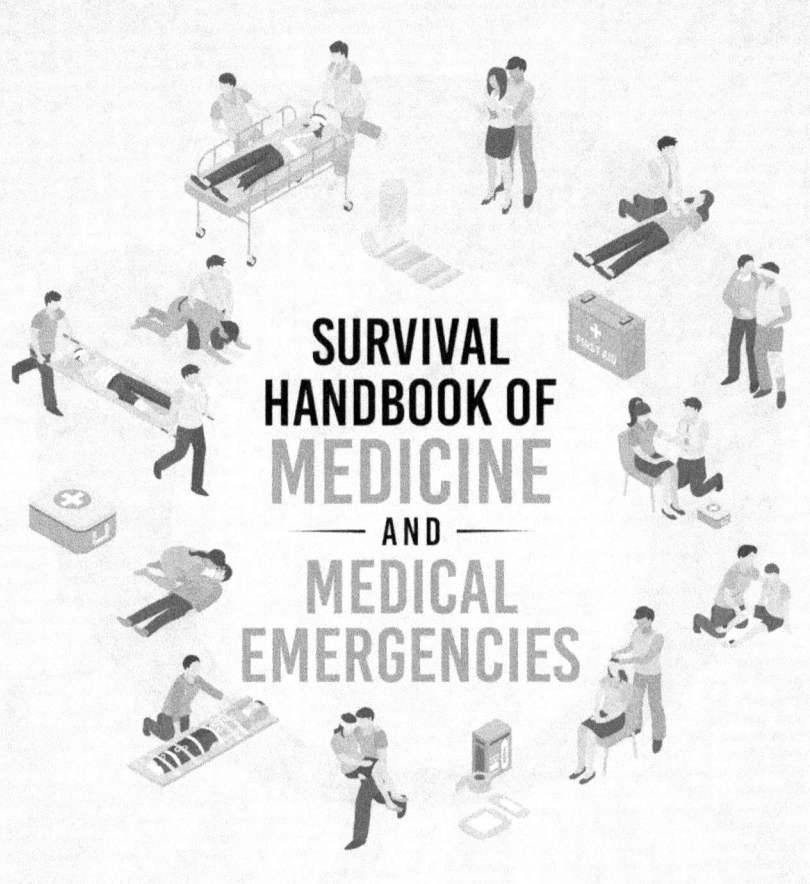

SURVIVAL
HANDBOOK OF
MEDICINE
— AND —
MEDICAL
EMERGENCIES

PREPPER'S OFF-GRID ESSENTIAL
GUIDE TO SAVING A LIFE

J. B. MAXWELL

INTRODUCTION

It is not the strongest or the most intelligent who will survive but those who can best manage change. –Leon C. Megginson

---

The feeling that we get while sipping our hot mugs of coffee and lounging on the couch with the warmth of a fire crackling close is that of belonging and security. We rarely consider what life would be like if we didn't have the conveniences of home and medical care. It's strange to think about how quickly things may go wrong and how we could be fighting for our lives alone. Don't you think that's a little scary? Many people have encountered comparable difficulties in the past and have triumphed. The fact is, the world is full of chaos, but the chaos can be managed. The only question is: Are you prepared?

Most of us have heard the story of *Robinson Crusoe* by Daniel Defoe. In simple terms, the whole point of the novel revolved around survival. Similarly, there have been numerous instances in a non-fictional reality where we have heard of people overcoming difficult conditions in the wilderness without access to medical assistance. In one such astonishing incident, Jose Salvador Alvarenga was discovered on the shores of the Marshall Islands' Ebon Atoll in recent years, specifically in 2014. He was said to have been wandering alone in the Pacific Ocean for 13 months. He had gone on a fishing expedition with a friend with extremely minimal supplies, but he had been blown to an unexpected location due to a severe storm. His boat was also damaged, and his partner died in the tragedy. Jose, on the other hand, managed to survive by eating whatever he could find, including fish, turtles, and birds. He also drank his urine to stay hydrated. The moral that we can take from this story is that if you have the desire to survive in a difficult situation and the necessary expertise to deal with medical issues, you can accomplish anything.

The various pandemics that have struck the globe over time, as well as natural calamities that have wreaked havoc in a variety of ways, have caused us to question our capacity as humans to a large extent. There are moments when we feel powerless and believe that modern medical treatments are the only option to ensure our long-term survival. Even if there is a desire to learn about medicine, there are complexities and problems associated with the educational approach. In emergency situations, it is all the more distressing for someone who wants to study the fundamentals of medicine to deal with medical emergencies before they've had a chance to be medically trained. More so, the sense of powerlessness that comes from seeing someone close to you suffer and not being able to help them, can become a deep-seated source of irritation for the rest of your life.

This book makes a concerted effort to assist anyone who has had a firsthand experience wishing to help a person in agony but was unable to do so due to a lack of medical knowledge. The main goal is to reach as many people as possible to teach them something that will help them survive in difficult circumstances, such as surviving in the wilderness without any professional medical assistance. The method-ical approach will provide a precise and in-depth understanding of how a person who has suffered a physical or medical trauma might receive lifesaving first aid help.

No matter how pleasant your current circumstances are, you are still vulnerable to life-changing events. As a result, upgrading your skills and preparing yourself for any type of threat is always a sensible move. Without access to a suitable professional space, you should constantly be informed on how the human body functions and the various therapies that can be administered. It doesn't matter if you're a novice or an expert; the drive to survive is what binds your will and, as a result, your actions. Learning the techniques and abilities associated with medicinal approaches can provide you with a sense of independence that can be a life-changing experience.

Nature's grandeur cannot be ignored, and the more we study about it, the less we believe we know about it. As a result, we all must work together with nature to nurture, protect, and learn from it. The importance of nature and its various manifestations in the wilderness cannot be overstated. When things go wrong, it may be as unwelcoming as it is challenging. An ultimate survivor is defined by the endurance required to remain safe and sound within their boundaries without the assistance of even the most remote civilization. The skills that you'll learn through this book will not only help you in the outdoors but will equally help you attend to anyone in dire condition.

What if I told you that if you develop your skills and become a medical asset, you can get through even the most terrible situations? Trust me; I've upskilled my knowledge by traveling to different regions of the Far East and discovering jewels of Eastern Medicine including Traditional Chinese and Ayurvedic practices, in addition to the knowledge I've gained over the years from studying within the domains of Western medicine. It is a fact that off-grid living provides a level of comfort and gratitude that is unfathomable. Off-grid living, however, also requires the tools and information needed to medically sustain yourself and those around you.

The primary purpose of this book is to make everyone feel secure and empowered. Because I've spent the last 10 years living in the wilderness and learning survival skills, I believe now is the ideal time to help those who, by choice or by circumstance, find themselves in the wild with no access to medical support. The forests and mountains have a lot to offer, and it's up to us to make the most of it while remaining environmentally conscious. I've witnessed firsthand how nerve-wracking some situations can be, and how, with a little tact, calm can be achieved.

Consider this scenario: You're on vacation and camping out in the woods with your family when you realize you've lost your way back home. The scenario becomes even more difficult for the person who is responsible for the other family members. In such a case, the pressure that builds up can aggravate the condition even more. However, if you have properly prepared yourself for wilderness survival, trust me when I say that you can easily aid your family members and yourself to overcome what could otherwise be a disastrous scenario.

Be it in the wilderness or even in the safe surroundings at your home, anyone could face any form of a medical emergency. Numerous people have preexisting health conditions and allergies which could affect someone's condition all of a sudden. More so, when you are outdoors away from the comforts of home, several causes could lead your health to fall in minutes. What if you are bitten by a snake or a dangerous insect, tumble off a cliff and break your leg, sprain your hands while carrying your heavy pack, suffer frostbite in the chilly mountain regions, or your nose suddenly begins bleeding and won't stop? The point is that medical emergencies can occur at any moment and in any location, and the only way to cope with them is to be prepared!

Many parents are concerned about taking their children on a prolonged vacation due to a lack of medical assistance near the vacation destination. Such anxieties are not uncommon; however, medical emergencies are also fairly uncommon. Therefore, such sentiments should not prevent a person from living the life of their dreams and embarking on a fun-filled adventure wherever. As a result, obtaining a basic understanding of medicine and its purpose, as well as a smattering of wilderness education, is a prerequisite.

Health and safety are the most important concerns for everybody, and via this book, I hope to take you on an enjoyable trip learning about medicine and outdoor survival techniques. I understand that many of us detest reading about medicine because of the complicated medical words. This will not be the case here; you will be able to learn about medicine simply, comprehend the power of natural medicine, understand human anatomy, common injuries, health difficulties, and the different ways to keep trauma at bay in such situations. As a result, with my comprehensive coaching, be prepared to meet a confident and knowledgeable version of yourself. So, let's get started on your journey to becoming a valuable medical asset in any situation.

11

ARE YOU PREPARED?

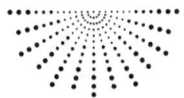

*H*ow many of us can say that we dreamed of being a doctor at some point in our life, or to be more specific, during our childhood? So much so that our excitement didn't stop with our confirmation given to the respective teachers at school; it also involved lugging the children's doctor playset around the house and placing a plastic stethoscope around our tiny necks, where we ended up taking everyone's pretend temperature. Furthermore, while many of us have achieved our goals, others have consciously chosen different courses in life that they prefer. The point is that no matter what job we all excel in, knowing a tad bit about medicine and comprehending how to function as a doctor in a medical emergency is something that we all need to know. The primary question remains: How can you be prepared for situations where there is no one to aid you, and you must treat and preserve another person's life as best you can? In other words, let me walk you through how to "be the doctor" in situations where you don't have access to any medical expertise.

We live in a time when technological and medical developments are at an all-time high. Professionally, people appear to be more preoccupied with work and all of the factors that go along with it. The rush and commotion of city life, as well as our roundtrip commute from work to the office, appear to have taken up the most room in our lives. We are all so preoccupied with catering for the everyday amenities that we forget that there is a world out there in the wilderness that we could visit eventually, either by choice or owing to circumstances. As a consequence, one should consistently be prepared for the best- or worst-case scenario. Not only should you be aware of the situation, but you should also be prepared to learn about medicine, medical emergencies, and, most importantly, how to survive in the wilderness. So, how can you be certain that you will be able to endure adverse circumstances? Well, that takes effort, and in this book, I'll explain to you how to educate yourself and keep abreast of some of the most prominent impediments that people encounter in times of hardship.

We learn the hard way, as they say, and the lessons we learn the hard way may well be the best teaching force for any of us. I've spent over a decade living outdoors, and there have been periods when I've questioned my ability to save those I care about from a potentially dangerous situation. Call it dread or the imprint that certain events left on my mind, nevertheless I decided to learn and study the extensive knowledge of medicine and medical emergencies, as well as to learn the ways of the wild via experience.

Allow me to relay an experience that I have personally witnessed. A group of our friends planned to go on a mountain hiking expedition. We were all looking forward to the experience, despite the difficult ascent. After days of planning and gathering provisions for the long trip and camp fun, we decided to start the adventure. It's hard to convey how exciting the road trip was. We rode across town to the mountain, singing and laughing the whole way. After nearly two days, we arrived at the base of the forest.

The zigzags of the seemingly never-ending trail toward the camp base were tiring, but we were all ecstatic. We were a group of five buddies from various professional backgrounds and had taken several such trips in the past. At the start of the trip, we were given the option of hiring a guide who was familiar with basic paramedic practices and the terrain. However, we refused since we did not want an extra person to make things odd for us while we were having fun. We were five physically robust men who were unafraid of the forest's mysteries. We were so excited that we immediately began our hike.

The first day was fantastic; we opted to camp near a valley that night and began preparing our tent. One of us commenced with the ropes and nails, while the others began preparing meals beside the fire. As we lay in our sleeping bags, gazing up at the sky filled with stars, it was a beautiful night. We fell asleep without even attentively fixing up the tent. We heard one of our friends yell in the early hours of the morning. A shout that could jolt anyone out of their slumber! We rushed toward him to figure out that he was indeed in some excruciating pain. All we could see on his calves was a red rash that looked like a bad bug bite. The place where we had put up for the night was an open space and we had not even imagined that he could have been bitten by a venomous snake in the dark.

Much to my dismay, I didn't consider that it could have been a snake bite at night. We'd heard of and dealt with insect bites before, so we assumed it was such a bite and started using whatever antiseptic cream we had on hand to assist with decreasing the bite's effect. With the daylight setting in, when I looked closely at the red part of his calves, I noticed that it was much more than an insect bite and was possibly a snake bite. It wasn't long after I told my buddies about my doubt that a panic set in. We were befuddled and terrified; we had no clue how to go about treating it, even as a first aid procedure. There was a problem, and our friend, who had been lying down since the dark, was dizzy, sweating, and appeared to be suffering a nervous breakdown. His foot had become fully swelled and inflexible. The agonizing scream that he let out is still fresh in my mind. We attempted everything we could to contact the ranger's post to plead for help. Fortunately, one of our pals was able to make contact with someone at the post and arranged an immediate medical rescue for our friend.

When we arrived at the paramedic station, the doctor noticed that he had become unsteady and that the venom had already caused severe harm to his system. He inquired if we had given him any kind of first aid, and just that question was enough to make my head spin! The point is that when the doctor explained how and what we should have done, even something as easy as taking off his anklet from his foot, something we had never considered, a tinge of guilt lingered in my mind. I believed that if I had some knowledge of recognizing a medical issue and taking the necessary steps to treat it or, at the very least, prevent it from worsening, my friend would not have suffered that miserably.

This encounter shattered my mindset to its core. Things that I had previously dismissed as insignificant were no longer so, which may sound philosophical, but being prepared, knowledgeable, and ready to be a trusted expert, is also a mindset. I was surprised to learn that after a snake bite, any tight objects in a person's clothing should be removed, that if vomit persists, the patient should be kept on their left side to ease them, that their breathing should be closely monitored, and that pressure pads could be used in many cases. I listened to all this information from the doctor and other staff, and only one thing struck my mind: I realized that we had not done a single action of the mentioned first aid steps to help our friend who was yelling even in a subconscious state with pain. This incident made me recognize the value of medical knowledge. I felt it was past due for me to devote more time to researching medical emergencies and wilderness survival. The feeling of helplessness when you see a living being in front of you in agonizing pain and you're unable to help them in any way is the worst that one can feel in their life. My point is, not everyone needs to learn the hard way; you can always be prepared for any difficult situation like this by expanding your knowledge. If we consider similar situations, we may be sure that there are many more people around us who have felt helpless or, more accurately, caught up in a medical emergency. All you can do as an individual is become self-sufficient to the point where you won't be afraid when you're out in the woods or if an emergency arises.

Medicine has been a boon to mankind's well-being as well as the well-being of all living things on the planet. My personal experience and close encounters with problems taught me the importance and depth of comprehending medical information, which fueled my desire to learn more about it. Let me take you through this journey of understanding medicine and its benefits.

A BRIEF HISTORY OF MEDICINE

Since the beginning of time, people have been surviving on this planet by overcoming a variety of conditions and ailments.

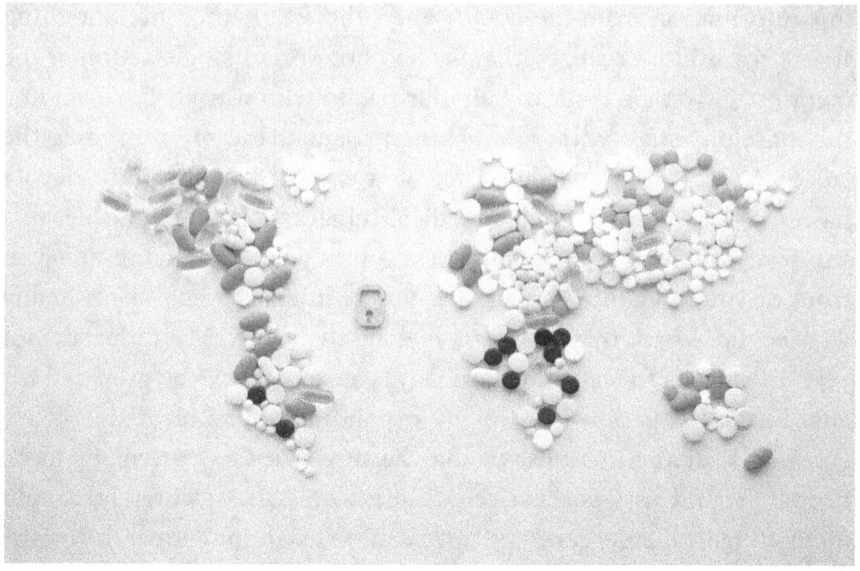

Though pinpointing a particular date to confirm the use of medicine to cure an illness is difficult, it is reasonable to assume that people have discovered a variety of therapeutic options since prehistoric times. With time, however, a progressive advancement in medicine began to emerge, paving the way for a variety of new treatments and approaches to cure diseases.

Medicine Before 1800

History is a vast subject and getting to the root of the origin of medicine can be a daunting task. However, with research over the years, along with evidence from pictorial art and archaeology of primitive surgical tools, there have been different perspectives on death and diseases. For example, constipation and bowel problems were considered a normal occurrence which was treated with the help of herbs. Plants were used for their medicinal values and were researched on a trial-and-error basis. Any sort of severe impairment was said to be caused by a supernatural force, such as an enemy's spell, a demon's curse, or furious gods who had projected something negative in the form of stone or worm in the patient's body and soul. Furthermore, they also utilized counter spells, medicines, suction, and incantations to heal both the body and the soul (Thompson et al., 2020).

According to Thomas (2012), to get the sickness out of the body, a surgical approach of drilling a 2.5 to 5 cm wide hole in the victim's skull was done using a trephine. Trepanning was used in Peru, the United Kingdom, France, and other parts of Europe. This type of procedure is evidenced by the discovery of a few prehistoric trepanned skulls. This practice is still used by a few Indigenous people in Melanesia and Algeria. Throughout the prehistoric age, the use of magic and religion in determining a treatment plan for various ailments was critical. Witch doctors and sorcerers can be considered the first doctors; they used plant-based medications and a variety of chants and dances to heal their patients. Folk medicines are perhaps the oldest feature of the healing art. Primitive physicians believed in holistic wellness and treated the body and the soul.

Medicine in Ancient Middle East and Egypt

According to Thomas (2012), the dawn of writing marked the onset of recorded history; clay tablets and other forms of records like seals and signs show how physicians in those days carried out their medical practice in ancient Mesopotamia and other regions. For example, the Code of Hammurabi, written by a Babylonian ruler in the 18th century BCE, is preserved on a stone pillar in the Louvre Museum in France. This code provides evidence of how harsh the laws of medical practice were during those days. Failure was punished severely under this code, which included legislation governing the medical profession. For example, if a patient died during treatment, the doctor's hand would be severed, and if the patient was a slave, the doctor would be responsible for finding another slave.

Herodotus, a Greek historian, said that every Babylonian could be considered an amateur physician. The sick would be laid on the street and every passerby could offer their knowledge or advice for the treatment. Divination was extensively used to predict the course of an illness by examining the liver of a sacrificed animal. Unfortunately, not much evidence or information can be found about Babylonian medicine.

Thompson et al. (2020) mentions that the preservation of mummies and the embalming of human bodies reveal a lot about the diseases that were common during the period. Tooth decay, bladder stones, bone tuberculosis, gallstones, gout, arthritis, and parasitic infections were among the ailments. There was no evidence of syphilis or rickets during that period. Further medical research leads to a study of Hebrew literature. Not much information about medicinal practice in Ancient Israel can be found in The Bible, but it does shed light on how Jews were pioneers of personal health and hygiene.

Traditional Medicine in Asia

For many years, India has been known for its history of medical expertise. Many of the sacred scriptures of the Hindu religion have been solid proof of the medical treatments that have existed for years. Fever, diarrhea, cough, skin problems, tumors, convulsions, and edema were some of the most common health issues treated throughout the Vedic medical period. Though the treatments were cutting-edge, their lack of detailed knowledge of human anatomy slowed them down. The Hindu faith outlawed the cutting of human bodies, which is why this became a worry for the evolution of therapeutic knowledge.

Thompson et al. (2020) suggest that dietetic approaches were primarily used to treat patients, while physicians used the five senses to detect ailments. Inhalations, cupping, and leeching were also used as treatments. It's amazing to think that major surgeries like caesarean sections and amputations were successfully performed back then. The doctors had a lot of experience cutting incisions and removing malignancies. Surgeons used precise punctures to remove toxic fluids from the body, especially the abdomen, in numerous cases. Additionally, many doctors had honed their stitching skills in preparation for the procedures.

China is also noted for its extensive medicinal heritage. The

Yellow Emperor wrote *Huangdi neijing*, which was regarded as literature on internal medicine. Only in the early nineteenth century were the Chinese introduced to European medicine. They believed that the human body should have an equal balance of elements: air, wind, water, and fire, so they used them as a strategy to cure ailments. The principle of Yin and Yang was also widely used in body healing at the time.

Mutilation of dead bodies was also highly disregarded in China and because of which, they, very much like the Hindus, had a setback on acquiring knowledge of human anatomy. However, during the year 1798 CE, a major epidemic swept the country and countless lives were lost. It was during this time that a writer of anatomy, Wand Qingren, studied human anatomy with the help of the remains of children that had been torn open by dogs (Thompson et al., 2020).

The Chinese had mastered the art of studying the pulse. They used some of the most effective treatments for a variety of diseases. They employed hydrotherapy, for example, to lower high fevers by giving patients a cool bath. A variety of medicinal herbs were used to relieve pain and heal ailments. Acupuncture is a treatment that is still used today, but it dates back thousands of years.

The Japanese were influenced by Chinese medical methods at the time. Only in the 18th century did medicine begin to show signs of Western influence. It's worth noting that the Japanese were responsible for the discovery of the bacillus plague in 1894, the discovery of the dysentery bacillus in 1897, and the discovery of adrenaline in crystalline form in 1901, which they used in the year 1918 for the first time on cancer that was tar induced.

History of Western Medicine

Early Greece marks the beginning of Western medicine. However, the transition from supernatural and magical beliefs and cures to science, did take a very long time. Greece was known for hundreds of temples and Asclepius was worshipped in those places. Numerous people went to these sites for incubation and temple sleep therapies.

The prevalent treatments then were more about diet, exercise, and baths.

Thomas (2012) suggests that by 460 BCE, the year when Hippocrates was born, treatments based on magic were all disregarded. He was later called the father of medicine. He believed in observing the patient in their environment and had a systematic way of diagnosis.

The century that followed Aristotle's work on medicine started to take full ground. He was also called the first biologist. It was his scientific studies that influenced scientific approaches over the next 2,000 years (Thompson et al., 2020).

Medicine During the 19th Century

As you move toward the 19th century, significant aspects that you will notice are the increase in the number of discoveries and also the practice by genuine doctors. By the beginning of this era, the human structure was an open book for medical practitioners. Microscopy and injections had already been invented and were used on a wide scale to treat different conditions. This century became adept with the knowledge of human physiology and germ theory. The discovery entailed the theory that infections were caused due to microscopic living organisms. It was also the age when the first vaccination was used.

The discovery and use of anesthesia was a remarkable achievement in the field of clinical medicine. It was during this century when Thomas Addison gave his name to some blood and adrenal glands disorders. This century did see a burst of eminent personalities who, for centuries, continued to inspire medical practitioners and researchers with their vast knowledge and ideas.

Medicine During the 20th Century

It was this century that brought in some of the best discoveries of treatment that changed many perspectives in the field of medicine. A worth mentioning development in the field of medicine that happened during this century was the study of chemotherapy. There was mass development in every field of medicine: infectious diseases, sulfonamide drugs, antibiotics, penicillin, antituberculosis drugs, immunology, vaccination, endocrinology, insulin, study of sex hormones, vitamins, study of malignant diseases, and surgery procedures, this era saw it all!

After World War II

Warfare does not provide a pleasant sight. It was after World War II that military surgery and many other advanced medical procedures came to the forefront. After the war ended, there were countless injuries and deaths. The doctors and nurses all returned to their normal civilian lives and continued to serve their respective countries by applying their experience of medicine learned on the battlefield for the benefit of others.

Gradually over the years, the development in the field of medicine reached a very high level. From complicated heart surgeries to major organ transplant treatments, the medical field has seen the widest range of advancements.

CONTEMPORARY DEMANDS

Change is happening every second, you may not realize the time slipping by, but yes, it is. As we have already touched on, the evolution of medicine and practices took place over the centuries. In recent years too, there have been remarkable advancements in technology and especially in the medical field.

ACCORDING TO THE GEORGE WASHINGTON UNIVERSITY SCHOOL OF Business (2020), "The healthcare industry is integral to the physical and economic health of every person in the U.S. Healthcare professionals are vital to enacting and enforcing policies and keeping the system running efficiently. Today, however, we need these professionals more than ever" (para. 1).

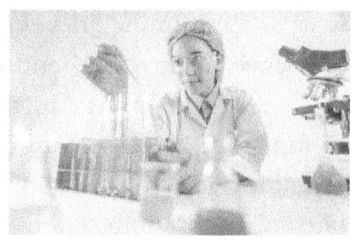

Dr. Mona Hanna-Attisha stated her profound concern about the level of lead in Flint's drinking water in the year 2016. Because of her efforts, she was able to make a significant difference in changing the water sources for drinking water, as lead was posing a significant health risk to children.

There continues to be people, belonging to all different age groups and having numerous health concerns. Due to that issue, combined with changing health policies, the need for a solid healthcare system along with more healthcare professionals is in high demand.

For example, here are a few reasons why there is a great need for more healthcare professionals than ever before.

Aging Baby Boomers

Baby Boomers are referred to those people who were born after the Second World War. The George Washington University School of Business (GW) (2020) reports:

Approximately 76 million people were born between 1946 and 1964, labeled the baby boomer generation, which was the largest in history. The oldest members of this generation reached social security retirement age in 2012; the remaining baby boomers will be of retirement age by 2030. Divide the 76 million baby boomers by the 19-year span of this generation to see an average of four million people retiring annually or nearly 11,000 people per day. (para. 11)

After retirement, the increase of baby boomers relying on Medicaid and Medicare is bound to increase and that can cause problems if there are limited medical resources. A bitter truth is that with the increase in age, there will be an increase in health problems. More facilities and insurance coverage will be required to run the system smoothly and, at the same time, give everyone proper medical access.

With more people reaching a health wise vulnerable age, the pressure of the healthcare department will double. Payment will be a big concern while the treatments are being done. Therefore, it becomes the responsibility of the health departments to keep an eye on the efficient functioning of the insurance systems. The main goal will be to provide the correct medical support to all aging citizens.

More healthcare professionals will be needed as the number of patients surges with time. Not just doctors and nurses, healthcare professionals like other staff, care providers, and professionals to check the IT systems will also be in high demand. People with experience who can add value and the benefit of their experience to the healthcare system should be hired. Expert professionals in technology and leadership should also be utilized as valuable resources ("5 Reasons Why We Need Healthcare Professionals Now More Than Ever," 2020).

Advancement of Technologies

The rapid boom in the advancement of technologies and especially in the medical field has caused several new innovative technologies and ideas to be used for the smooth functioning of the healthcare system. One of the most astounding inventions has been that of home-care monitoring gadgets like the blood glucose and heart rate monitors.

As per the report by GW (2020), "The global home-care diagnostics and monitoring market is predicted to grow 8.71 percent between 2016 and 2020. Technology is the driving force behind the increase" (para. 30).

There are advanced patient monitoring systems from a remote distance and wireless sensor technologies that have made medical practice quite efficient. The doctors and the medical practitioners can observe and guide their patients from any location in the globe. The wireless sensor technology gives comfort to the patients to move around free of any wires that would otherwise hold them back.

With the increase in technologies, there will be a bigger increase in the demand for more healthcare professionals and especially professionals of healthcare informatics. A higher number of people will be required to fill the needed posts that will help make the healthcare system a better place for everyone and most importantly, the patients in need.

Growth of Biopharmaceutical Industry

According to the annual report by Evaluate Pharma, there has been an increase of 6.3 percent in the rate of growth of the pharmaceutical industry in the year 2022 (as cited in "5 Reasons Why We Need Healthcare Professionals Now More Than Ever," 2020). The demand and supply chain concept works in this case, for instance, with the increase in the number of patients with severe illnesses, there will be the need to produce more drugs and other medical items required for the treatment.

With the increase in the production of biopharmaceutical products, there will be a need for a large number of people who are skilled and educated enough to work for the company. The requirement of medical professionals will be even more. The healthcare system requires professionals who are fast and at the same time highly efficient. People who know chemistry, biology, and clinical research are some of the examples of people who could benefit from getting a job in circumstances like these.

Transformation for the Better

Healthcare is a field that requires a lot of external support as well. Support in the sense of better healthcare policies and advancement of technological aspects. Politics and their different roles in the implementation of various policies have great potential to bring a massive change in society as well as the system. No matter which party forms the government, the main idea is to put together ideas and thoughts of diverse and responsible professionals for the overall development of the medical industry.

Over time, different policies keep on coming to the forefront, but the main point is to understand how well-educated and skilled professionals get opportunities in the healthcare field.

According to GW (2020), "Specialized education is the first step to achieving success in healthcare. Healthcare professionals who want to get involved in the business of healthcare may consider an MBA program that specializes in this industry" (para. 35). However, with every policy and change that will get enforced, there will be a huge requirement of professionals in the healthcare department, especially in the following:

- Healthcare policy jobs: With the recent changes in the healthcare system of the United States, there will be several organizations that will require professionals who have good experience with the health policies. With regards to the policies, these professionals must be able to check if proper protocols are being followed or not.
- Consulting healthcare jobs: Numerous private firms and providers are unable to hire professionals adept with the healthcare policies. These companies get external help from healthcare consulting companies as they have access to the financial modeling and data that is advanced, and which cannot be reached by other organizations.
- Government policy jobs: This is a career that is highly significant as the professionals have an opportunity to influence the policy before its creation. The government employs such healthcare professionals to collect data about the success and failure rate of the ongoing healthcare programs and also asks for suggestions if there are any to help people and the health of the entire community.

When taken a closer look, you will realize how important a healthcare career can be for you and how it can benefit people in need.

Healthy Competition

Healthy competition is the key to success in any field. If professionals are more enthusiastic about their tasks and career, then there will be healthy growth that can lead to many advantages.

The GW (2020) reports that according to an *Academy of Management Journal* article published in the year 2010, "Competition leads to enhanced creativity when professionals are excited about the task they are performing. When the same people are anxious or nervous about their tasks, competition is more likely to lead to unethical behavior" (para. 24).

A drive to be the best in your career can lead you to find ways that can help you hone your skills even more. For example, according to reports by the Harvard Business School, an increasing number of people are now pursuing an MBA degree to become doctors (as cited in "5 Reasons Why We Need Healthcare Professionals Now More Than Ever," 2020). Similarly, the already experienced doctors are taking up specializations and choosing their desired field more rapidly.

With the rise in awareness about the healthcare system and the careers around it, more people will understand that there are several other options for becoming a medical professional.

WHY IS IT IMPORTANT TO BE PREPARED?

Difficult situations will not be announced before they hit you hard. Especially if the emergency is medical, if you are not prepared, it can lead you to a big problem. Situations may get tense very fast, and if no action is taken immediately, then there will be chances that the situation of concern may rapidly become more serious.

For instance, you may be out in a park with your family or friends and all of a sudden, your friend's finger gets cut open by a sharp tin, but you have no clue as to what action you must take. Now, this can be bad as the cut may lead to severe infection and loss of blood even before the medics arrive.

However, if you've had your share of knowledge about medical emergencies, then you'd know what to do immediately to stop the excess blood flow. The first step that you would do is clean the wound with some water and apply pressure on the finger to keep it intact and also to stop bleeding. By the time medics arrived, you would have taken good care of the situation.

Therefore, you can see how even in the simplest of situations, your preparedness with medical knowledge can help lessen someone's pain and more so, even save lives.

1 2
BECOMING A MEDICAL ASSET

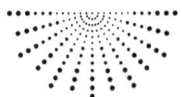

$\mathcal{F}$rom the dawn of civilizations to modern times, one thing that has always been the most beneficial for every living being on earth is medical care and preparedness. As you already know by now, even the tiniest of health issues can cause severe threats to lives. Negligence and a laid-back attitude toward health can cause serious harm in the long run. The truth is, you have people you care about all around you, like your friends, family, and loved ones. Just the thought of any of them, including you, falling victim to some kind of health emergency can be nerve-racking in itself. The truth is also that if medical care is given to anyone at the right time, a huge problem can be lessened or even prevented.

However, as an individual who understands the importance of grave circumstances and the benefit of the medical system, you must first ensure yourself that you can be prepared and help others, especially when you are on an expedition to outdoor terrains.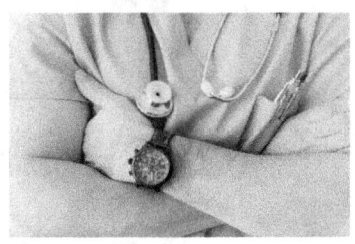
One of the first steps that you must take before going to the wilder-

ness is to understand every member's fitness level: if they have any pre-existing health conditions like cardiac issues, breathing issues like asthma, allergies, etc. Another important factor that you must check is if the weather is suitable. Having clear knowledge of the upcoming weather forecasts is mandatory. Last but not the least, you must be prepared, and so should you prepare your fellow companions as to how to handle the situation if anyone gets hurt during the adventure. After all, if it's you that is injured, having given some prior knowledge to your group, might very well allow them to properly help you.

BASIC MEDICAL EDUCATION

Once you've made up your mind to become a medical asset, you need to understand what medical knowledge that you must learn.

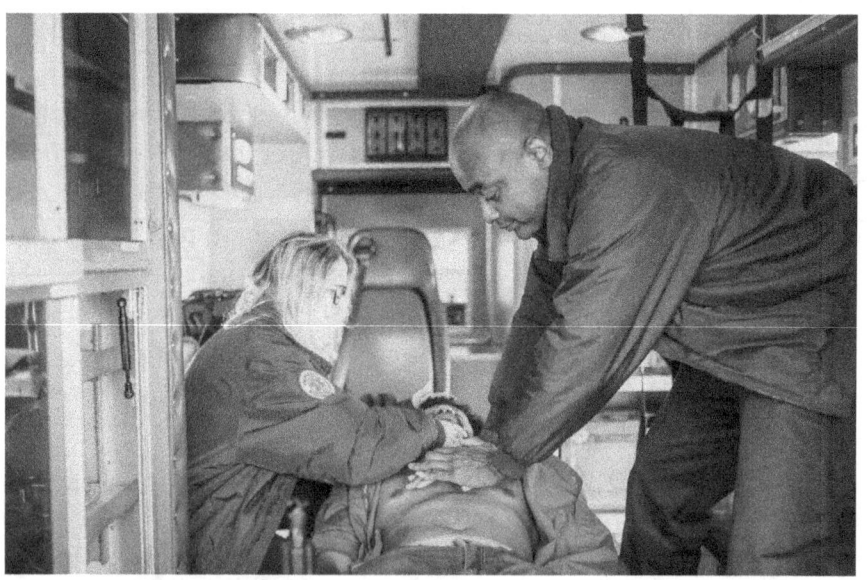

Cardiopulmonary Resuscitation (CPR)

CPR is a life-saving emergency procedure. It requires a series of chest compressions along with artificial ventilation. The main purpose of this method is to keep brain function, breathing, and blood circulation in place until medical help arrives. It is an easy-to-learn process and can be beneficial in a huge way.

Set a Splint

This is a method of setting up a stabilizing mechanism in an emergency to help a broken arm or leg stay in place. During an emergency, it can be made of any available sticks and clothes. This process helps the bones to remain intact and prevent excess pain that can be caused by movements. This is a highly recommended method that could be used if someone in your group ends up breaking their bones. You may be in the wilderness, far from help, but this technique can keep the fractured and broken bone at rest for some time.

Burn Treatment

Treatment of burns can be tricky as there are three different degrees of burns. When a person gets burned, you will have to determine the burn level. For example, if it is just a first-degree burn, then make sure to apply a soothing ointment on the affected areas and cover it with a thin gauge. If the burn has resulted in some blisters and has created a bit of swelling, then that can be termed as a second-degree burn. In this case, you will have to run it under cold water and apply an ointment over it. However, the third-degree is the most acute of all and will require the immediate help of a doctor.

Spot a Concussion

A concussion can occur as a result of a blow to the head caused by a hit or fall. Particularly in the outdoors, you must be able to determine whether or not someone has suffered a concussion. Examine the pupil to check whether it has dilated and ask the patient if they are dizzy or experiencing any discomfort. If a serious concussion is not treated promptly, it might cause permanent brain damage.

Heimlich Maneuver

Choking is hazardous, especially if proper first aid is not provided. The Heimlich Maneuver is a technique for helping a choking person push out whatever was restricting their airways by giving an abdominal thrust above the naval area. You should fist your hands and press into the upper naval area back and forth until the impediment is gone. You can perform this maneuver on yourself by using a hard, solid, stationary item (chair, counter, log, rock, etc.) and pressing your body forcibly against it.

Stop the Bleeding

This is one of the topmost medical aids that you must be aware of. A person could excessively bleed and lose their life quite quickly. You must know how to make a tourniquet to combat rapid blood loss.

By following some of these important first aid techniques you will be able to save your own life as well as the lives of many others.

WILDERNESS BASIC MEDICAL EDUCATION

One of the primary motivations for embarking on a journey into the wilderness is to immerse oneself in nature while remaining as remote as possible from the hustle and bustle of cities and towns. I'm sure there aren't many things that can provide the same level of tranquility as the wilderness. Several people yearn for serenity as well as a profound desire to enjoy the outdoors while also feeding their curiosity about wildlife.

The farther you travel into the wilderness, the farther you will be from any medical facility or emergency department. Staying outdoors has many advantages, but one of the most severe disadvantages is the difficulty in seeking medical treatment. As you travel through the deepest reaches of the mountains and forests, the chances are very high that you will be bitten by a swarm of insects and may even come face-to-face with an animal or two. Tents can be tough to live in, and the weather can be harsh at times. In such a situation, just imagine someone on your team facing some major health issue; the probability will be high that they will suffer, but if you have adept knowledge about how to deal with medical issues, then that can be a great advantage.

Your Immediate Actions

There are many aspects that you'll have to be careful about while going out in the wilderness alone or with a group. However, if you have even the slightest suspicion that something is going wrong, and the nearest emergency services are a long way away, a few first aid basics should be added to your other important first aid actions (Schimelpfenig, 2020):

- Try to evaluate the person who is in pain.
- Understand the scene.
- Identify what could be life-threatening.
- Ask for the patient's medical history.
- Conduct a head-to-toe exam and look for any threatening signs and symptoms.
- Check the eyes for signs of a concussion.
- Immediately start thinking about what the medical care plan should be for the patient.
- Prepare for immediate evacuation in case the medical relief people arrive.
- Continuously make an effort to check the condition of the patient.

These are some of the most important steps that you can follow to ensure that the patient is safe and conscious.

First Aid in the Wilderness Can Be Tricky

When considering first aid in the wilderness, keep in mind that it will be considerably different from what you would do in a city or town with medical services nearby. Here are some of the factors that influence wilderness treatment:

- When you witness someone suffering or being harmed, the first thing that comes to mind is to call 911! That's not going to work in the woods. The terrain is difficult, and the woodlands are dense, so getting medical help will be next to impossible. As a result, if you find yourself in the middle of a medical emergency while backpacking, you must be prepared to care for the patient and keep them safe for a long time, at least until a medical rescue team arrives. It could take days, weeks, or even months at times. Therefore, it is up to you to take all the necessary first aid actions.
- To stay prepared in the event of a medical emergency in the wild, have the most important medicines and equipment with you at all costs. Carry your medical gear with you at all times and be prepared to treat a patient with whatever supplies you have on hand. For example, at a hospital, when a patient who is dehydrated and has diarrhea, they are given IV fluid therapy. In the wild, though, the situation will be different. If you don't have access to an IV, you'll need to give the patient plenty of water. You might also use electrolyte powders or salt and sugar water instead.
- In the outdoors, communication can be the most difficult. Without a doubt, technological and network coverage have improved in many challenging regions, but owing to network unavailability or fluctuating coverage, even sending a text message, deep in the woods could take a long time. As a result, if you're in the middle of nowhere and have a medical emergency, things might get complicated quickly because though you'll be carrying your cell phone, you could find it extremely difficult to call people for help.

- When you're out in the woods, the weather may have a big impact. Though various weather forecast applications clearly show you the approaching weather of a location ahead of time, you can still be subjected to many untold complications caused by sudden changes in the air. You will have to make it in tents and eat and drink the few supplies that you've carried. Therefore, if at night you get very chilly, you will have no option like a bigger blanket to ease you. All that you will be able to do is light a fire and drink some hot tea to keep yourself warm.

Therefore, if you've decided to have an adventure-filled life in the wild, then these are some of the things that you must be aware of and should be ready to live with.

Protocols to Follow While Giving Treatment in the Wilderness

The treatment process of a patient in the wilderness can be quite different from that in a medical room. A few vital methods of treatment procedures and a few protocols that you can follow before and while treating a patient are listed below as guidance (Schimelpfenig, 2020):

- Always check the area where the patient fell sick or got injured. There might be clues as to what could have caused the injury or health hazard. For example, take a look around to see if there are any traces of poisonous creatures or plants that could have caused an adverse reaction. Also, if the patient gets hit by something or is found in a slippery or high place, make sure to take them to a safe and clean area.
- Look for others who have been injured, too. There might be people who assume they are fine and could even look fine, but in reality, they could be suffering from trauma or concussion.

- Always ask for consent to go ahead with the treatment—if the patient is in a conscious state.
- If the patient is unconscious, make an effort to bring them back to consciousness.
- Treat every unknown disease as infectious. Always wear a mask, and a pair of gloves to keep yourself protected at all times.
- Check how serious the injury or illness is and accordingly, devise a plan to start the medical procedure.

Having followed the above protocols, you can perform the following essential first aid actions following the ABCDE rule (Schimelpfenig, 2020):

- A: Always check the airway. Examine the entire mouth to see if there are any obstructions.
- B: Go near the chest and check if the patient is breathing normally or not.
- C: Ensure to check the patient's pulse and also look around if there are any signs of internal or external bleeding.
- D: If the patient hurts the spine, there will be chances of a temporary disability. Protect the spine area in case you cannot find the cause of the immobility.
- E: Exposure of injuries is a must, open the tight clothes of the patient and check if there are any injuries.

As a result, by checking various indicators of the patient, such as heart rate and peculiar odors, as well as excessive bleeding and signs of the skin turning pale or blue, you will be able to understand the reasons for health problems and, as a result, be able to treat them on time, even in the wild.

TOP TIPS FOR WILDERNESS MEDICAL EMERGENCIES

As an outdoor enthusiast, I've had my fair share of emergencies. There have been numerous incidents while trekking through snow-capped regions to dry forest areas that have taught me how to deal with medical issues in the wild. However, here are some of the most prevalent medical hazards that can occur outdoors at any moment.

The truth is that there is not as significant of a difference as you might think between the medication used in the wild and that used in health facilities. Similarly, patient behavior does not depend on location. The patient's personality has a role in dealing with medical issues, whether they are outdoors or confined to a hospital room, since some people get terrified at the sight of a drop of blood, while others may treat even a major cut not so seriously. In both circumstances, treating such people can be dangerous.

However, the setting may be so bizarre that stabilizing a tough medical emergency in the wild will require a lot of focus and tenacity.

According to Decker (2018), here are some tips that could help save lives in the wilderness:

- Snake bite: If a snake bites you, immediately try to take a picture of the snake to figure out the venom type. Wash the bite area and bandage it. Never try to suck the venom out. Immediately rush the patient to the hospital for antivenom treatment.
- Hypothermia: If someone is hypothermic, ensure that the person is wrapped up with a space blanket or a foil. Provide warm compress throughout the body of the patient. If the condition persists, you can use the technique of your body heat treatment. Give the patient frequent hot water or tea.
- Open scalp wound: In case of a major accident and the scalp opens wide, until the medical rescue team arrives, you can

tie the hair of the patient across the wound to keep it in a stable position.

- Insect bites: Always use an insect repellant when you are outdoors. However, use Plantago (plantain) to help soothe the irritation. It can also be helpful for sunburns.
- Diabetics: Always carry honey to treat low blood sugar. At times when people start hiking, they tend to forget to eat on time and prolonged aerobic exercise lowers blood sugar. Honey is a great way to raise glucose levels and can be rubbed on the gums if the person is unresponsive. Honey is also said to be a great antibiotic.
- Check dehydration correctly: Hyponatremia is a condition in which the body's sodium level goes below normal. Hyponatremia affects a large number of people. This has been observed during expeditions through the Grand Canyon, where people mistakenly believe they are dehydrated and drink large amounts of water (Myers & Hoffman, 2015). As a result, you should always check the color of your urine to see if it is overly concentrated (the darker the urine, the more dehydrated you are). If a person is dehydrated, provide them with not only water but also sufficient nutrition.
- Injured bone: When you encounter a situation where a patient has probably broken or fractured some part of their body. Then, make sure you immobilize them. Make use of any stick or rods that are available nearby to give support to the affected part.
- Purify water: In the wilderness, the best way to purify water is to boil it. Make sure that you boil for a little longer than the boiling point to ensure that all harmful bacteria is killed in the process.
- Use feminine hygiene products: Products like sanitary pads can be of great help while out in the wild. They can be used to give padding to an injury or to help seal a wound. Tampons on the other hand are perfect to stop nose bleeds.

- Carry a headlamp: This should be on the priority list of the accessories needed for a wild expedition. The nights can be very dark and with many things to carry and do, a headlamp can free your hands and be extremely easy to use.
- Altitude sickness: This can be a serious issue for someone who faces challenges in high-altitude regions. The first step for you would be to make the patient descend to a lower altitude region.

We have discussed a large number of possible medical emergencies and the ways to overcome them all. However, the point is, there are important accessories that you should always have by your side while on an expedition in the wild. A few of the most essential tools that will be of great help to you in the wilderness as mentioned by Buer (2016) include:

- safety pins
- trauma shears
- wilderness guidebook
- thermometer
- antibiotic ointments
- 2nd skin dressings
- bandages
- sam splint
- gloves
- antiseptic towels
- povidone-iodine solutions
- wound closure strips
- cotton swabs
- tweezers
- scissors
- band-aids
- 12cc irrigation syringe
- 1-inch cloth tape
- sterile scrub brush

- 4-6 inch elastic wrap
- 4x4 sterile gauze pads

With the correct tools in place, any health problem can be given good medical support.

KNOW YOUR SURROUNDINGS

Your confidence is what will enable you to conquer even the most difficult conditions in your life. When you're on a wilderness adventure and you're going to new places, you should always make sure you know what the landscape is like and the methods to deal with situations related to it.

HEAT

According to a report by Lipman et at. (2014), in the last decade, more than 600 people succumbed to death due to causes related to excessive exposure to heat. Heat-related illnesses are very common, and many people suffer due to them. It is a condition in which the body temperature of a person reaches a very high level resulting in organ damage, including the brain, kidney, heart, and even muscles. Some of the heat-related issues are hyperthermia, heat cramps, heat exhaustion, heatstroke, and heat syncope. Few drugs and medications are also considered to be a big cause for heat-related illnesses such as antipsychotics, antihistamines, alcohol, amphetamines, alpha-adrenergic, beta-blockers, benzodiazepines, calcium-channel blockers, cocaine, clopidogrel, diuretics, laxatives, phenothiazines, thyroid agonists, tricyclic antidepressants, and neuroleptics.

In their article, Lipman et al. (2014) provide some of the ways to reduce the body temperature of patients:

- One of the most common ways to reduce the body heat of a person is to take them to a shaded area that has access to cool air. Most suitably if the room or the place is below the temperature of 20°C (68°F).

- Hydration is the key to curing water deficiencies and can substantially reduce hyperthermia. However, ensure that the patient does not get overhydrated as that will cause pulmonary edema.
- Immersion in cold water can be a very effective way of reducing body temperature. It can substantially prevent heat stroke.
- Evaporative cooling is another measure by which heat of the body can be reduced if no immersion facility is available. This is done by loosening the clothes of the patient and sprinkling cold water onto the body to reduce body heat.
- Ice packs and chemical packs are some of the most convenient ways to reduce body heat. You can apply them externally to the skin in the neck and groin regions to reduce excessive heat.
- Ice towel application is another very simple way to help reduce body heat.
- Antipyretics are used to treat elevated temperatures.

There are innumerable ways to counter illnesses caused by excessive body heat, and one of the best ways is by making the body cool down using natural methods that are easily accessible.

COLD

Issues like hypothermia, frostbite, and many other injuries are problems that affect people who venture out in the wilderness during excessively cold weather. Cold weather can harm the health of some people even if they do not go outdoors.

Different individuals will have different levels of endurance to cold. Hypothermia is a condition in which the body temperature falls below 35°C (95°F). Some of the common symptoms of hypothermia are exhaustion, extreme shivering, feeble memory, slurred speech, fumbling hands, drowsiness, and lack of coordination.

Hypothermia, if left untreated, can result in heart and breathing system failure, as well as death. A person with hypothermia usually is not aware of their condition right at the beginning. Due to this reason, people may become perplexed in their behavior as a result of this illness.

If you face a situation where someone is suffering through this condition, you should take the following action ("Hypothermia," 2020):

- Handle the patient with extra gentleness. Do not massage or rub the patient as vigorous movement can cause cardiac arrest.
- Immediately take the patient to a warmer place. However, if moving is not possible, then keep the patient in a horizontal position and cover with warm blankets.

- Remove wet clothes immediately.
- Cover the patient with warm clothes and blankets.
- Monitor heart rate and breathing continuously and if by any chance you realize that there is no pulse, then immediately start with CPR.
- Use a warm compress to increase the body temperature of the patient. Apply the warm compress on the chest, neck, and groin. Refrain from applying a compress to the feet and arms because doing so can cause the cold blood to circulate back to the brain, lungs, and heart. This can cause a serious drop in the body temperature and that could be dangerous.
- Give warm beverages to the patient, but only do so if the patient is conscious.
- Do not use hot water bags or heating pads directly to the patient's skin because that may suddenly heat the body and could cause irregular heartbeat.

Therefore, be careful next time when you deal with someone suffering from hypothermia.

Frostbite is another severe problem that people face while exposed to extremely low temperatures. When the skin and underlying tissue get injured due to the cold and the damage is not very permanent, then that condition is called frostnip. This condition can be treated with the help of warming the affected areas. However, if the condition is severe, then it is frostbite.

Numbness, waxy-looking hard skin, muscle stiffness, prickling feeling, reddish or bluish skin, and blistering can emerge when rewarmed. These are some of the key indications and symptoms of frostbite. If the swelling and agony worsen, as well as if you develop a fever, you should see a doctor immediately ("Frostbite," 2021).

According to the Mayo Clinic (2021), until the medical team arrives you can attend to the condition of frostbite by following a few measures:

- Remove wet clothes from the body.

- Cover all the affected areas and keep them safe from the cold wind and air.
- Do not walk if you have frostbite on your legs.
- Do not try to roughly move the parts of your body affected by frostbite.
- You can use a painkiller to help deal with the agony caused.

ADAPT TO ALTITUDE

Without visiting a region with steep terrain and greater altitude, treks and hikes just feel incomplete to those of us who love an outdoor adventure. Most people who enjoy the concept of discovering new locations and nature must have felt the need to adjust to the altitude at some point in their lives. However, as beautiful as the higher terrains can be, some people can face equally bigger health issues due to high altitude.

High altitude illnesses are common and there are some very effective ways to prevent such symptoms. There has been a surge of traveling to higher peaks in recent years. For instance, a UK-based company offered around 93 expeditions to Mount Kilimanjaro in just 12 months. However, with the increase in such expeditions, the chances of more people falling sick due to high altitude will also escalate. Similarly, cases from the Rocky Mountains and European Alps have reported similar illnesses all caused due to altitude (Shah et al., 2015).

While hiking on a steep slope or toward a higher altitude, many times you may not realize whether it is just the normal panting that is happening due to the climb uphill or whether you are having a breathing issue. In such a case, always note a few key signs and symptoms ("Altitude Sickness," 2020):

- headache
- dizziness
- nausea

- vomiting
- inability to walk
- coordination problem
- feeling of suffocation
- persistent cough
- disorientation
- chest congestion
- fatigue
- breathlessness

Once you've identified any of such signs in yourself or anyone around you, make sure to take the following steps ("Altitude Sickness," 2020):

- Every sickness that is related to shortness of breath, nausea, vomiting, and headaches should be considered to be altitude sickness until proven otherwise. If these signs persist, immediately stop the climb and descend to a lower altitude.
- While going on a hike uphill, always follow the graded ascent rule; do not over climb in one day.
- If any of the people with you feel any discomfort, address their issue immediately; do not wait for their condition to worsen.
- Keep an eye on the patient.
- Generally, within 1-2 days most patients start recovering. However, be extra alert.
- For headaches, you can administer Ibuprofen and acetaminophen (Tylenol). Always be careful about the correct and safe dosage.
- Do not allow the patient to have any sleeping pills.

Climbing uphill can be a stressful task under normal conditions, but when the harsh climate of the hilly areas is added on, then there can be more stress. Due to such exertion, you may experience discomfort and some signs of illness. Take any sign seriously and stop hiking immediately if you feel any kind of discomfort in your health.

NATURAL DISASTERS

Natural disasters are reported to cause roughly 500 deaths each year in the United States alone (Cormier, 2017). In the sphere of disaster management, disaster preparedness and healthcare resources frequently fall short. Staff members in the hospital, family members of patients, and, most crucially, the patient in question, are all at risk in the event of such a situation.

Anyone can become a victim of a natural disaster, no matter how much people plan as per weather reports and other forecasts; the fact is that elements of nature work in their bizarre way and sometimes can be very unpredictable.

When a natural disaster strikes, no one is spared. Therefore, the most important point is that there should be adept planning and preparation for any case that is related to a natural disaster. Here are a few tips by which there can be a more planned approach toward managing a natural disaster situation:

Communication

Problems that people face as a result of organization-wide actions and policies can be solved with clear communication. Many times in the past, organizations have hesitated to provide precise information to the public. This approach is disadvantageous since it can lead to a slew of misunderstandings and, more importantly, plenty of unfounded speculations. There will be widespread panic, especially after catastrophic events, but this can be alleviated and calmed to a large extent if healthcare services make an effort to explain the situation to the public. People will respond positively to information provided by a healthcare authority.

Even within the organization, there should be clear-cut communication between the members and staff. Everyone should be informed about the ongoing situation. Effective implementation of protocols and plans can be done only by having everyone on the same page. Every top-tier department, including management and government affiliates, should be aware of the current state of affairs.

Training

When a natural disaster strikes, the healthcare system should be more prepared than any other department, as there will be a risk of numerous people getting injured. Just because a flood has not happened in the last two decades does not mean that it will not hit any time soon. Preparation is key, and training is the only way in which a huge part of the situation can be handled in times of crisis.

A laid-back attitude by organizations and their employees can be harmful as one will never know when an emergency can hit a place. Therefore, all the healthcare staff should be given intensive training to understand how to manage things during times of natural crisis. Healthcare organizations should conduct emergency preparedness drills, coordinating with local emergency response agencies and the public whenever possible.

Technological Protocols

Hospital management and employees have discovered that access to patient data and hospital documents becomes inaccessible after a natural calamity, causing considerable damage to the hospital's property as well.

Not only should the tangible room where important and valuable documents are kept be improved, but the data stored in various files should also be stored appropriately to save important information.

Healthcare Leadership

Hospitals and other medical facilities are so preoccupied with their day-to-day tasks of treating innumerable patients that the healthcare administration staff frequently overlook outdated catastrophe plans. Medical facilities, for example, should be self-sufficient to give quality medical care and emergency treatment to persons injured or traumatized, even in the event of a disaster. This way, they may gain the trust of the community while also serving them, which will be extremely advantageous to their ability to generate more revenue from the service.

The essential point is that hospitals deal with difficult situations and emergencies regularly, but all higher authorities should keep natural disasters and protocols for dealing with them as a top priority as well. If there are any approaching disasters, every department must be well versed in their preparations. They should constantly be prepared to meet any crisis with tenacity and efficiency.

Knowledge of Assets

Hospital authorities must be prepared for emergencies of all kinds of natural disasters as well. When a natural disaster occurs, it becomes a horrendous task for the government officials and hospital authorities to attend to every single person affected or hurt. There will be a massive rush in the hospital that may make it impossible to rely on any outside help. Keeping in mind such situations, it is imperative for healthcare organizations, especially hospitals, to be aware of the supplies and assets that they have.

MAJOR EVENTS

Major events are disasters, causing unimaginable destruction to the people, community, and environment. Some examples of events with prolonged risk of threat include radiological, biological, and chemical disasters.

Radiation

History has seen some of the cruelest and painful radiation disasters. The majority of these have been caused by severe nuclear power plant explosions, which were primarily triggered by accidents. Whatever the origin, the consequences of such incidents have resulted in damage that is beyond repair. For example, the Windscale Fire Nuclear Disaster in the United Kingdom in 1957, the Three Mile Island Nuclear Accident in Pennsylvania, USA in 1979, and the 2011 Fukushima Nuclear Disaster in Japan ("The Five Worst Nuclear Disasters in History," 2014).

Aside from major catastrophes, it is also a reality that radiation exists in the form of background radiation, which is produced by natural minerals.

Kim (2018) asserts that "for reducing radiation exposure, there are three principals: time, distance, and shielding" (para. 1). However, in the event of a calamity caused by an accident or even a terrorist strike, there are a few steps you can take to keep yourself safe:

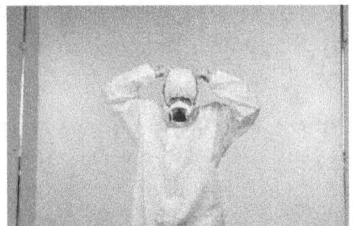

- Understanding the three aspects of time, distance, and shielding can be very useful.
- Under unavoidable situations, limiting the time of radiation exposure can be a good way to minimize the effect of radiation.
- Maintaining a distance from the source of radiation can help in reducing the effect.
- Creating a barrier of lead, water, or concrete can minimize the penetration of x-rays and gamma rays drastically.
- In case of a sudden radiation emergency, stay indoors (a concrete building is best), and close all the openings like windows and doors.
- Stay in the sheltering place until and unless the authorities pass on information to get a contamination screening done.

Radiation exposure can cause serious health hazards like radiation sickness, skin burns, heart issues, and also cancer. Therefore, whenever there is a chance of you getting exposed to any place or object that could be contaminated with radiation, ensure that you follow strict measures and keep yourself and others around you safe and sound.

Biological

Biological hazards can cause major life risks to humans and animals. Toxin, microorganisms, spores, fungi, and viruses are some of the examples of such substances. Biohazards can affect any environment and include pathological waste, human body fluids, animal byproducts, sharps, infectious waste, human blood, and recombinant DNA and RNA. Here are a few best practice methods that you could follow to stay safe in an environment plagued with biohazards (Burns, 2009):

- Universal precaution: Treat every situation with grave concern. Deal with every potential biohazard like blood or any other infectious item as dangerous.
- Gloves: Clean your hands and check if the gloves are in good condition. Check for leakages or anything inside that could harm your health. Thoroughly clean your hands and then wear your gloves. Do not touch anything with bare hands, and when you are done, carefully dispose of the gloves in a safe biohazard bin.
- Body protection: In cases of extreme contamination, ensure that you have personal protective equipment (PPE) like a proper body jacket, apron, or other suit ready. Ensure you wear them at all times and discard them well after you are done.
- Face protection: Ensure you always use eye goggles, a face mask, and most importantly a face shield at all times.

- Clean-Up: Cleaning up is a process that is vital for decontaminating an area. Always carry a biohazard bag and kit in situations where you will need to do a lot of clean-up. Put on your gloves and protection gear while going through the process. Use disinfectants and sometimes a bit of bleach to clean places that have been contaminated.
- Sanitize the equipment: Clean the space thoroughly and then use a professional person to sanitize the area and the equipment that cannot be discarded.
- Decontamination: After you've done your work, clean your hands with antiseptic wipes and let them air dry. Go to a washroom and wash your hands and the parts of your body that have been potentially exposed with a strong soap.

There has been an increase in the improper disposal of trash products in recent years. If those who work with biohazards are not attentive in classifying waste products as biohazards, it may generate problems for those who work in the cleaning department. Keep an eye out for sharp edges that could be contaminated. Make sure you break them down safely and dispose of them in biohazard garbage bags.

Infections relating to biohazards can be dangerous. However, by understanding the risks involved and by spreading awareness, a lot can be brought under control.

Chemical

Chemicals can be dangerous if they are not handled with care and extreme caution. Substances that are non-biological that can pose threat to human and animal life are chemical hazards. Unfortunately, chemicals have become a big part of our daily lives. These days, there is a presence of chemicals in a majority of things. From the food that we eat to the cleaning agents that we use in our homes, all contain some chemicals.

There are three main ways in which you may come in contact with chemical hazards: food and water, air, and touching a potential chemical hazard. Here are a few ways by which chemical hazards can be prevented by following a few measures:

- Prevent chemical accidents by being extra cautious, avoiding mixing of chemicals, and storing the chemicals in a place accessible to only authorized personnel.
- Prevent fire accidents caused by chemicals by keeping them in a fireproof storeroom.
- Prevent spillage by being very careful. If there are any spills, make sure to get it cleaned thoroughly by following the right measures.
- Dispose of unused chemicals carefully. Do not throw them in places that could be dangerous to the water supply and wildlife, too.
- If you find someone is poisoned, immediately call the poison control authorities.

In the event of a chemical hazard accident, do not panic! Read and follow the instructions given by the authorities and follow every single step as mentioned. Follow the news and radio and stay sheltered until they declare the situation is under control.

With the wealth of information available on healthcare facilities and how to become a medical asset, it's clear why medical knowledge is so important for survival. Whether you believe in living in the wilderness like me or not, there is always the possibility that anything could go wrong in your everyday life. The guidance that is provided in this chapter can be helpful in unforeseen times. You may be out in the wild and by knowing how to tackle every situation, you will be confident to take any journey without a hiccup. The confidence that you get as a result of being knowledgeable is something that you cannot compare with any other knowledge. It is the thought that you know your loved ones and the people around you are safe that gives a great sense of life satisfaction. As a result, comprehending problems and generating strategies to get out of them can be a huge accomplishment. You can save the lives of many people by educating yourself as a medical asset.

13

THE POWER OF NATURAL MEDICINE

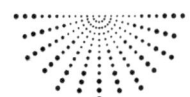

The enigma around planet earth and its rich composition of plants and living organisms will always remain a beauty. Throughout the ages, humans and animals have survived some of the toughest challenges that civilizations face. Natural calamities like floods, droughts, landslides, volcanic eruptions, and at times even meteors, have ravaged many parts of the world. Epidemics and pandemics have been very prevalent over the course of evolution.

With time, there has been massive development in the field of medicine and technology. No matter to what level the allopathic range of medicine and its treatments have reached, the importance of natural medicine cannot be overlooked. If you think  about it, how have people and animals been surviving numerous illnesses since the beginning of time and also before the discovery of modern medicine? This proves the point that there is a plethora of natural herbs and remedies that have the power to solve and cure many diseases and ailments. The health benefits that can be found in natural products and the medicines created from natural plants and other sources can be said to be humongous.

You must be confused as to how plants and herbs that you hardly know the names of can be used for medicinal purposes. If you are out in the wild, you may not be equipped with the best medicines all the time; it is in a scenario like this that nature and natural medicine can save your life. By acquiring correct knowledge about natural medicines, you will know what to do next time you need some relief.

NATURAL MEDICINE IS THE WAY!

The modern world is exposed to the dangers of chemicals and pollution. At times like this, contamination of any sort can cause serious life-threatening problems. The healthcare industry has regularly seen a huge influx of patients suffering from new and different types of diseases. There are many cases where allopathic medicines can prove to be too strong to the body and mind; they may heal you but can at the same time have the potential to cause innate harm if not taken in the correct dosages. However, there is a reduced chance of adverse effects with natural medicines.

Natural medicine follows the principles of self-healing and vitalism techniques. A naturopathic doctor will almost always ask you to not get parallel treatment for the same condition from an allopathic doctor. The reason why contemporary medicines and other medical procedures are encouraged to be avoided is that they believe that the body takes its due course of time to heal and is capable of self-healing provided the right methods are used ("Naturopathy," 2021).

It may take a while for the person who has always been exposed to allopathic treatments to understand the benefits of natural medicines. This makes it essential for you to understand the details of natural medicines and their benefits to help guide others who are in need of natural based care.

Benefits of Natural Medicines

Apart from the systematic and holistic healing process used to balance out the entire system, including body and mind, there are other essential reasons why opting for natural medicines would be a good decision. The Institute for Natural Medicine (n.d.) discusses the need for and some of the benefits of using naturopathy:

- More affordable: Healthcare costs in the United States have been on a rise for quite some time. At such a time, policymakers have been urging medical practitioners from various fields including naturopathic doctors and primary care doctors to play their roles in making an effort to provide valuable service to the people in terms of their health and well-being. The main priority of the healthcare system should be to look into the health of people apart from just providing the treatments.
- Not just the policy-related matters, it has been seen that natural treatment has a wide range of options that can be way less in cost than in comparison to conventional methods. Naturopathic treatments believe in curing the root cause, therefore, the cost for medicines and surgeries focused on treating just the symptoms can be greatly reduced. Healthcare and insurance costs that are often used for the treatment of cases resulting from adverse reactions of conventional medicines are also substantially reduced.
- Reduced side effects: Natural treatments are said to cause zero to a minimal level of side effects. Natural medicines are made from herbs and everything that is of nature. There are no harmful chemicals involved because patients usually do not experience any adverse reactions from their usage.
- Health promotion: At times when the conventional method of treatment and medication seems to fail, numerous people start looking for alternative medicine. It is in such a situation when natural medicines enter the scene. Natural medicines are said to be non-toxic and safe which makes it one of the most desired methods of treatment. Natural

techniques of healing are a great means of treating pain. Hence, a holistic approach to treating pain is often adopted.

- Easier to obtain than prescription medicine: Requiring a prescription to acquire medication can be expensive, tedious, and difficult, demanding doctor visits, regular tests, and continual efforts with refills and insurance. In comparison, natural medicines are easily available and do not cost as much.

- Natural healing: Natural medication is all about treating the entire mind and body together as one. This technique makes an effort to find the underlying cause of any health condition. The practitioners of this method think that the body has the potential to self-heal. With much time given, natural medicines can show their effect in curing a person for better health.

- Strengthen the immune system: There are numerous herbs and natural items that are beneficial to strengthening the immune system. It is your immune system that protects you from any form of illness that enters your body and fights harmful health threats. Some of the herbs and medicines that are natural are said to boost energy and at the same time, increase the efficiency of your immune system.

- Naturopathic medicines are available for any age: In conventional methods of treatment, many medicines are prescribed with keeping in mind the age of a person. People suffering from exhaustion, stress, and other related disorders are most likely to opt for a treatment that can have no side effects in the long run. People of any age can opt for a natural medicinal treatment that cannot just cure their sickness, but can at the same time cause no damage to their organs.

What Are Herbal Medicines?

Herbal medicine is the application of plants and herbs to make medications by integrating their therapeutic properties, scent, and even taste. A majority of people turn to herbal medications from conventional treatments in order to gain better health benefits and improve their holistic well-being. Teas, fresh plants, dried plants, plant extracts, pills, and capsules are all commonly used forms of herbal medicine.

There is a widespread fallacy that all medicines labelled as 'natural' are entirely safe for wellness. This isn't always the case, though. One concern with herbal medicines is that they are not subjected to the same rigorous standards of testing and trial practices as conventional approaches.

A few herbs, such as ephedra and comfrey, are thought to be hazardous if used incorrectly. As a result, you should strive to seek a trustworthy recommendation from a natural doctor, and also inform your health practitioner before testing any of these plants as medicines.

What Are Naturopathic Medicines?

Natural medicine refers to the natural remedies that are used to cure and heal the body. There are quite a few different types of naturopathic therapies that include acupuncture, exercise, massage, natural counseling, and most important of all, herbs. The United States was introduced to naturopathic medicine in the 1800s. However, it cannot be denied that some of the treatment procedures are derived from age-old practices and knowledge.

It is considered that naturopathy belongs to the era of 400 BC, and it was Hippocrates, a Greek philosopher, who ciphered the principles of the practice. The practice of natural medicine is considered to be a wide range of pseudoscientific methods and is often termed natural, self-healing, and non-invasive. The practitioners of natural medication are referred to as naturopathic doctors and they have to undergo professional qualifications and obtain required licenses to practice their medical knowledge ("What is Natural Medicine," 2021).

There are numerous kinds of practitioners specializing in their respective fields and because of which, generalizing them into one particular type is a difficult task. The treatments done via natural methods can range from homeopathy, open quackery, and also to psychotherapy which is a mainstream treatment ("Naturopathy," 2021).

It has to be noted that natural medicine is derived from age-old practices and studies, the philosophy of this field relies on the knowledge of old folk medicine and practices. It cannot be called evidence-based medicine (EBM) like that in the case of allopathy. There are still some practitioners who believe in EBM and try to work on the principles of evidence and proof.

TAKING CARE OF THE SICK

How a person is taken care of is what speeds or slows the recovery process. In recent times, what people generally do when they feel even a slight sickness is to pop a pill and then let the medicine take its due course in relieving them from the symptom.

Understandably, this is not a sound practice. Taking unprescribed medicine every single time you suffer from a slight headache is not the right approach toward your overall health and can actually cause internal damage in the long run. This should not just be the case with conventional medicines; while having herbal medicines, too, you must realize that consultation with a good practitioner is always the best to do.

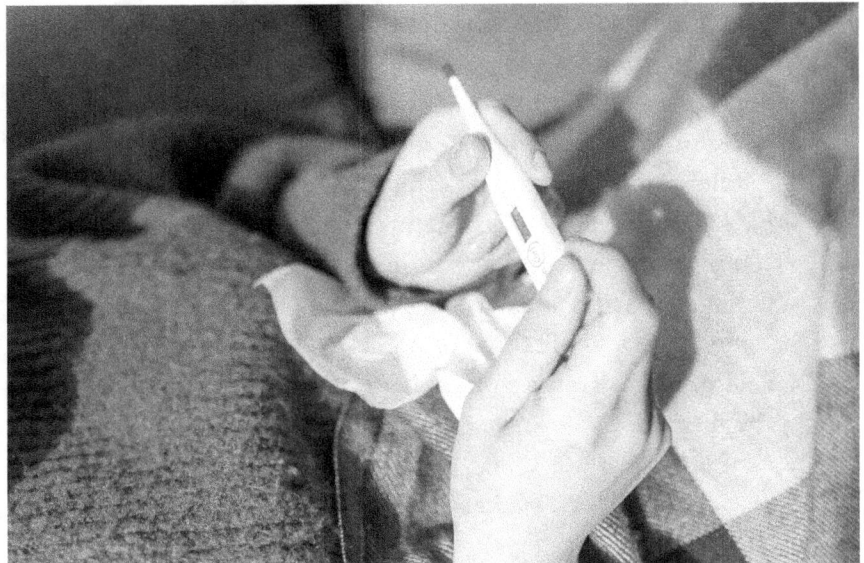

However, there are a few home remedies that you could try instead of consuming medicines of any form right away.

Home Remedies for Sore Throat and Cough

When you have that itch in your throat and a cough that seems to incessantly bother you, there are numerous home remedies that you can attempt before trying out other conventional medicines. As a professional medical provider, Sloun (2015) states:

I wish that being a doctor meant that my family and I would never get sick. Unfortunately, viruses, bacteria and other sources of illness do not discriminate based on profession. Here's what's in my toolkit to keep us going in sickness and in health. (para. 1)

Sloun (2015) discusses natural remedies that can be used for treating some health illnesses:

- Tea: Consuming hot tea can give you instant relief from an itchy and sore throat. There are ingredients called slippery elm and licorice that have throat-coating properties that have beneficial effects in reducing irritation of the throat.

- Honey: Said to have antibiotic and throat-coating properties that have been proven to cure cough and throat problems, you can take it with a spoon or mix it in warm water or tea. Be careful to not give honey to infants and toddlers as it might cause serious harm.
- Elderberry syrup: This is a remedy that has been used for centuries to cure colds and influenza.
- Echinacea: This can be used as a remedy to cure a cold by using drops and pills containing it.
- Pelargonium: This is a plant that is used to cure colds and coughs.

Home Remedies for Sleep

Sleep issues can create serious havoc in your daily life. Instead of trying strong medications that can be harsh for your system, you can try these two methods (Sloun, 2015):

- Tea: Try sipping some chamomile tea before your sleep time. It will relax your system and soothe your mind, which will, in turn, encourage a night of good sleep.
- Lavender: Lavender is known for its soothing properties. It can be used as an aromatherapy oil to calm your mind and relax your body. It has a relaxing effect that will induce you to sleep in no time.

Home Remedies for Digestion

One of the most common health issues that people face is concerning their digestion. Whether it is the food that is consumed or the quantity that is taken in, digestive problems can be painful and annoying. Here are a few remedies that you can try the next time you feel your stomach is a bit upset (Sloun, 2015):

- Ginger: This has been used by sailors for a very long time to cure nausea due to seasickness. It has medicinal properties and can be helpful in motion sickness and stomach problems. You can consume ginger by making small tablets of it at home or by drinking it in the form of tea.
- Probiotics: These are yeasts and bacteria that are termed "good bacteria." These are great for your digestive system and can help prevent stomach issues, especially diarrhea caused by the use of antibiotics or infections. These can be found in local stores in the form of miso paste, yogurt, kimchi, kombucha, and other fermented foods.

Home Remedies for Anxiety

Anxiety is an issue that countless people suffer from. Here are a few methods that you can use to lessen its effect:

- Do simple breathing exercises for a while every single day and while doing so, be grateful for everything good in your life.
- Slowly inhaling and exhaling breathing exercises can help calm you down instantly.
- Nourish your body with healthy food and juices.
- Keep your mind fresh by feeding in positive thoughts.

Home remedies can be highly beneficial in helping relieve some pain and health problems. Next time you feel uncomfortable with some sickness, you should head into your kitchen and grab some of those home remedy ingredients instead of popping those strong pills. Here are a few ingredients that have immense healing properties ("Home Remedies: What Works?" 2021):

- Peppermint: Mint has remarkable healing properties and has been used for generations to cure stomach-related issues. Irritable bowel syndrome that causes gas, diarrhea, bloating, cramps, and constipation can be relieved healthily by the use of some peppermint oil.

- Turmeric: Turmeric has been used as a medicine in many ways for numerous years. It is used in cuts and wounds as an antibacterial measure. It is also said to help in fatty liver and arthritis conditions. It has been used to cure skin problems like rashes and ulcers.
- Garlic: It is widely believed that people who consume more garlic are less prone to certain types of cancer. Many use it to lower cholesterol and blood sugar as well.

Amazingly, you can see how many different natural items can prove to be beneficial for your entire health. The first step toward good health is acknowledging the fact that taking care of your mind and body is the key method. Negligence of health can lead to disastrous problems. However, with the correct use of herbal and natural medicines, you can prevent many issues concerning health.

Medicinal Plants for First Aid

Medicinal plants in the countryside, and even in some parts of the bigger cities, are not scarce. Nature has provided a plethora of plants and herbs that are highly effective at healing when used properly. According to clinical herbalist Steve Byers (as cited in Sarnacki, 2019), you do not need a ready-made band-aid to heal your wounds, you need to be connected to your land and use your resources effectively. Sarnacki (2015) talks about how these few medicinal plants that can be lifesaving when you are in the outdoors and have no access to any conventional medicine:

- Old Man's Beard: This plant is known as bearded lichen and is traditionally used for having antibacterial properties. It can be found throughout North America and its scientific name is *Usnea*. It is soaked in water and used on wounds, and it is also dried and powdered to be used externally.

- Cattails: This plant can help relieve burn wounds and is found widely in North America.
- Jewelweed: This plant can help in case of itching and pain caused by stinging nettle and poison ivy.
- Common Plantain: It can be mashed, made into a poultice, and used on wounds. It is found in North America and is known for its properties to soothe the skin.
- Calendula: Calendula is also found in North America. It can be used as tea and can help in washing wounds. It is used extensively throughout the world to cure skin rashes, dry skin problems, bee stings, and inflammation.
- Common Yarrow: This plant is remarkable in stopping blood. It is one of the most kept in the first aid kit of wilderness explorers. It can be used to cure burns and wounds, and can at the same time, treat headaches and colds.
- Arnica: This plant is found in North America and is known to help in bruises and sprains.
- White Willow: The bark of this tree is said to have anti-inflammatory effects. It helps reduce headaches and other pain.
- Goldenseal: This plant is used to treat ear and skin infections.

As you can see, nature has provided remedies for every possible health issue, many of which are discovered and many of which are yet to be known. There is a magnanimous range of plants, and especially medicinal plants, that most of the time people hardly bother to understand or contemplate their value.

As a person who has seen a larger part of the world through the wilderness, one thing that has been a learning lesson is that nature can always be used in your favor in terms of medical emergencies. You will just have to be sure as to which plants to use precisely to help resolve a medical urgency. However, with the required knowledge, almost anyone can start on their journey to venture out in the wild without any fear or confusion.

14

UNDERSTANDING THE HUMAN ORGANISM

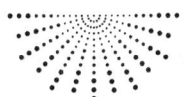

*U*nderstanding the basics of survival and especially if you want to become a medical asset in the long run, help save lives. Additionally, at the same time to survive in the wilderness, you must understand how the human body works.

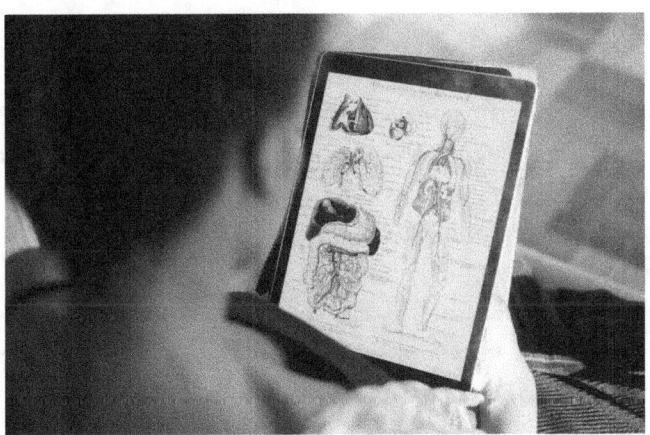

How many times do we even think about our body and wonder how it is designed and how it functions in the way it does? Hardly does anyone give a thought about these things. However, the main idea is that gaining vast knowledge about human anatomy will help you in many situations. With an adept knowledge of the human body, your problem-solving skills will be higher when it comes to anything related to humans and that is essential for survival.

OVERVIEW OF HUMAN ANATOMY

Human anatomy is a complex subject to understand fully, and many medical institutions require multiple semesters to complete this subject. Every bone, muscle, organ, blood vessel, and cell have their unique part to play in the design and function of the body. There are approximately 206 bones in the human skeleton, 600 muscles, 78 organs, and numerous cells and blood vessels ("Bones, Muscles, and Joints," 2012). The word anatomy means the study of the structure of living organisms and is a branch of medicine and biology. Therefore, studying and having clear knowledge of anatomy and an understanding of how all the major systems work is of prime importance for the study of medicine.

Skeleton

Skeleton is responsible for protecting all the vital organs and at the same time, giving a firm posture to the human body. The human body is moving all the time, whether walking, running, exercising, and even when resting, the human body is always functioning.

Fibrous connective tissues called ligaments are responsible for attaching the bones. Joints can be classified into two different types, movable and immovable based on their function. For example, movable joints can move and are flexible whereas immovable joints are not movable and are also called fixed joints.

Muscles

Muscles are tissues that assist the bones in locomotion. It is the tendons that connect the muscles to the bones. Movable bones function with the help of joints, but joints and bones cannot budge without the assistance of a muscle. Contracting and relaxing actions are used by muscles to propel the body forward.

Divisions of Human Anatomy

There are two important divisions in human anatomy:

- Macroscopic or gross anatomy: This division deals with structures that are large and that are visible to the naked eyes. This branch of study shows the location of all the human structures and also explains in detail how each structure is connected with the other.
- Microscopic anatomy: This division deals with the structures that are at the microscopic level, which means they are not visible to the naked eye. It is the second division of the study of human anatomy. It mainly studies tissues, veins, microscopic arteries, capillaries, and nerves, along with their position and role in the organ system.

Human anatomy is a vast subject to study. Therefore, a proper understanding of the different body parts can be studied in a systematic way to make it a bit easier.

Human Body Parts

The head, neck, and limbs are connected to the torso. Four limbs are perfectly postured to fit in the torso of the body. The shape of the body is given by the skeleton and is composed of bones and cartilage. All the organs of the body are placed inside the skeleton. Some of the relevant organs are the brain, heart, and lungs. The spinal cord is a very important component that connects the body with the brain.

Human Body Structure

The human body is composed of different cavities that are responsible for housing various organs. The three most distinct cavities are as follows:

- The cranial cavity: This cavity is responsible for the protection of the nervous system. It is a location in the skull where the brain and other important parts of the nervous system are firmly and safely placed. It acts as a shield to protect the brain from any external jerk or blow.
- The pleural cavity: This cavity is responsible for maintaining the optimal function of the lungs. It also acts like a protective wall that helps the lungs stay safe even when there is heavy breathing.
- The abdominal cavity: This is a cavity that is responsible for housing and giving external protection to the organs like the liver, spleen, and intestines.

These different cavities act as a support system for all the essential organs.

Circulatory System

The cardiovascular system of the human body is also referred to as the circulatory system. The heart and blood vessels including arteries, veins, and capillaries, are all an integral part of this system. There are two types of circulation systems:

- pulmonary circulation
- systemic circulation

The circulatory system is responsible for providing nutrients and oxygen to all the cells in the body. It also plays an integral part in removing waste and carbon dioxide. The heart is the organ that functions as a pumping machine to deliver oxygenated blood and deoxygenated blood to the required locations. Thus, it is also referred to as the transport system of the body.

Digestive System

Food is essential for the human body to function, and it is the digestive system that has the job of breaking down food and helps in supplying nutrients. These nutrients are further used by the body to repair its cells and for growth.

Descending in order, the most important parts of the digestive system are:

- mouth
- teeth
- tongue
- esophagus
- stomach
- liver
- pancreas
- gastrointestinal tract
- small and large intestines
- rectum

As simple as it may sound, the digestion process starts from the time you chew your food in your mouth. The saliva helps to soften the food which makes it easier to swallow. The chewed food then moves through the esophagus and enters the stomach. It is in the stomach that the most important part of the digestion takes place. Certain acids and enzymes are powerful enough to turn all the food into a paste.

After the process of the stomach, the food is moved into the small intestine. This is where food is digested even more because of a strong secretion that is released from the liver and pancreatic enzymes. It is at this stage that nutrients from the food get absorbed into the system. All the leftover material is moved to the large intestine where liquid is removed. Finally, all these materials are passed on through the rectum as waste in the form of stool.

Reproductive System

Commonly known as the genital system, the reproductive system is a vital part of the human body. It is the most essential section that comprises all the external and internal organs that are responsible for reproductive function in humans. However, there are a few distinctions between the male and female reproductive systems. Understanding both reproductive systems will give you a transparent view on the distinctions and how each organ works toward the reproduction process in humans:

- Female Reproductive System: This is composed of ovaries and the uterine tubes. Ovaries are responsible for the production of female eggs called the ovum. It also produces a hormone called estrogen. Uterine tubes consist of fallopian tubes and oviducts. Also known as the womb, the uterus is a pear-shaped organ where the fetus grows. The cervix is between the uterus and the vagina. The vagina is where the male reproductive part, the penis, enters the female body during intercourse, delivering sperm that travels up through the cervix. This also acts as an exit for the fetus during the time of a normal delivery.
- Male Reproductive System: This consists of testicles that store sperm that are essential for reproduction. These organs are oval and are placed in the scrotum. Vas deferens are muscular tubes located near the testis. This is one of the most important ducts belonging to the male reproductive system. Every time sperm is created, fluids produced by the seminal, Cowper's, and prostate gland merge. The Cowper gland then helps in increasing the volume of the semen that is required for lubrication during the process of coitus.

The reproductive system is an integral part of the human body system. It is because of this system that humans can generate offerings and carry on with the conventional process of life.

Nervous System

The nervous system is a complicated network of cells and nerves that are responsible for transporting signals from the brain and the spinal cord to all the different parts of the human body. The nervous system can be divided into two integral parts:

- Central Nervous System (CNS): All the voluntary and involuntary actions that a human body is capable of doing are guided and controlled by the CNS. Every part of the body is connected through axons. The CNS consists of the forebrain, midbrain, and hindbrain.
- The forebrain consists of the hypothalamus, thalamus, and cerebrum. The cerebrum is said to be the largest part of the brain. Understanding languages, thinking, perceiving, motor functions, emotional, and even sexual functions are controlled by this part of the brain.
- The midbrain is associated with the brain stem, and it is because of this part that visual and auditory functions can work smoothly.
- The hindbrain is that part of the brain that connects the spinal cord to neurons.
- Peripheral Nervous System (PNS): This system comprises all the nerves that branch out from the spinal cord and brain. It consists of two systems, namely the somatic and autonomic nervous systems.
- The main function of the somatic nervous system is to pass all the sensory and motor impulses from the CNS and bring them back again. This system is linked with limbs, the skeletal system, and other sensory organs.

- The primary function of the autonomic nervous system is to relay impulses from the CNS to the muscles and other organs of the body. This system requires the support of the person. It is because of this system that the body can protect itself from any sudden blows, attacks, and also during conditions where the body temperature gets exceedingly high.

The nervous system is highly significant in the process of the normal functioning of the body. It is by which the mind and the body work in sync together.

The human body has a very unique way of functioning, especially with the presence of numerous cells and different organs; the entire process seems to be more complicated to understand. Through a proper study of the anatomy of the human body, and by under-standing how major organs and muscles work, you can find it much easier to practice any medical treatments on anyone if need be during an emergency. It is necessary to understand how a particular system works because only with the optimal knowledge about the human body can you move ahead with your goal of becoming a medical asset in the future. Let us now dive into details about a few categories of illnesses and the first aid approaches to deal with them all.

RESPIRATORY ISSUES

Respiratory issues are often not taken seriously by many people. For example, they walk for a mile and start panting or they may take a hike up the mountains and find it difficult to breathe. In both cases, they will try and blame the exercise or the altitude for their breathing issues. Though they may be correct in their opinion, the fact is that breathing problems have to be taken seriously and taken care of in time before any complications crop up.

Breathing problems can be categorized into the following types:

- short of breath

- gasping for air because of inability to take deep breaths
- feelings of inadequate air supply

Breathing difficulty can be caused due to internal issues. There-fore, ensure you go through a thorough check-up if you notice any of the above symptoms regularly.

HEART ISSUES

Cardiac issues can be lethal if not taken care of at the right time. Some of the most common heart issues that you can encounter are a heart attack, sudden cardiac arrest, and an angina attack. Heart attacks can take place at any time, but there are a few symptoms that you have to be mindful of understanding.

One of the most prevalent symptoms of a cardiac arrest is that of chest pain. The pain generates in between your chest and then moves toward your neck, jaws, ears, arms, and wrists. The pain can be acute and initially, it will start with a mild ache. Sensations like heaviness, tightness, squeezing, constriction, and burning are some of the most common that you will feel. Most often, people confuse it with the sensation that is felt during heartburn or indigestion.

The following are some of the indicators of a cardiac arrest ("What to Do in an Emergency," 2020):

- chest pain
- pain in arms, jaw, neck, abdomen, and back.
- feeling sick
- sweaty
- looking pale
- restlessness and panicky
- breathlessness
- wheezing
- coughing
- rapid heartbeat, palpitation
- feeling dizzy

There are many cases where a woman or a diabetic may not feel any chest pain at all. However, if you spot any of the symptoms, then make sure you consult your doctor immediately.

Actions to Take During a Heart Attack

Call your local emergency number immediately! Make the patient sit and rest for some time until the ambulance arrives. Aspirin is said to be beneficial at such times but if you do not have it around, do not go searching for it as that time may be crucial not to be wasted. If you get an aspirin, chew a 300 mg aspirin immediately. Do not let the patient or even if it is you, stay alone until the ambulance arrives ("What to Do in an Emergency," 2020).

Once the paramedics arrive, give them all the medical details about the patient including allergies and medical history.

URINARY TRACT INFECTIONS

Urinary tract infection (UTI) is very common in people of all ages. This type of infection can occur in any part of your urinary system. The urethra, ureters, kidneys, and bladder can all be targets of this infection. Urine is said to contain no bacteria and is a byproduct of the kidneys. The process by which kidneys remove excess water from the waste material is what forms urine. Bacteria can enter the system from external sources and can cause inflammation and infection in the urinary tract.

Some of the most common symptoms of a UTI are:

- urinating frequently
- feel like urinating now and then
- pain during urinating
- lower back and side pain
- pain during intercourse
- fatigue
- pain in the penis

- fever
- vomiting
- confusion

It is believed that one in five women contracts a UTI every single year ("Urinary Tract Infections," 2010). UTIs are diagnosed by urinalysis and urine culture tests. Antibiotics are the most common way to treat UTIs. Some of the common antibiotics used are amoxicillin, doxycycline, quinolones, sulfonamides, nitrofurantoin, and many others. It is important to keep your body fluid up and not dehydrate yourself so, drink a lot of water.

GENITAL ISSUES

Infection of the reproductive organs can be termed genital issues. Such infections can affect all genders. However, let us take a look at what genital issues are for the male and female reproductive system distinctively.

Female Genital Infection

Female genital infections can be felt in the form of vaginal and yeast infections. If you have a vaginal yeast infection, you could try a home medication by using a non-prescription drug like tioconazole, clotrimazole, or miconazole. If your symptoms persist even after a few days, make sure to consult your doctor immediately.

Here are some of the ways to handle the situation:

- If you are pregnant, ensure that you consult your doctor immediately if you notice unusual vaginal symptoms.
- Avoid intercourse during the time of infection as that might cause you immense irritation and pain.
- Do not scratch the infected areas no matter how bad they itch.

- Apply cold compress to the affected area, cold baths can also help.
- Warm baths are said to help heal some pain and itching.
- Wear cotton-made loose fitting clothes at all times.

Most vaginal infections clear up within a span of a few days. If you notice any of these symptoms, then visit your doctor soon and get a thorough check-up.

Male Genital Infection

Men are prone to genital infection as well. They are susceptible to yeast infection which can cause situations like balanitis. Swelling, pain, bruising, and inflammation are some of the common signs of male genital infection. There are quite a few home treatments that can be used to promote healing which can cure the condition in a matter of a few days. However, if the pain and swelling persist, it is always recommended to visit a doctor very soon.

If you would like to give it some time and try some home remedies, then here are a few methods:

- Rest is essential and while doing so, ensure to protect the sore area.
- Use ice packs to help reduce the swelling. You can apply the pack for around 15 to 20 minutes many times a day.
- Wear loose, cotton underwear to help protect the bruised area.

By following these simple methods and at the same time, maintaining good hygiene, such infections can be put aside.

BLEEDING

You might get caught in an accident or cut by even a sharp tiny leaf. Whatever the reasons may be, bleeding is something that everyone should know how to handle. Here are a few steps by which you can control bleeding:

- If you encounter someone who is bleeding profusely, make sure that you remove their clothes and debris from the areas of the wound. If large objects have seeped into the body, ensure not to remove them as doing that can make the person bleed more.
- Wear your gloves before cleaning up the wound.
- Place a sterile bandage on the wound and firmly press it to stop the bleeding.
- Place the patient in a comfortable place and position.
- If the blood seeps through the gauze, then do not remove it. Instead, add more bandages on top of it.
- Use a tourniquet, if you know how to use it, as it is said to be effective in controlling heavy bleeding.

Even after you apply all the first aid procedures, if the patient does not stop bleeding, then you have to somehow take them to the nearest emergency facility or call the local emergency number.

You will experience a feeling of worth and contentment when you help save someone's life. Understanding the human body and how it works is fundamental knowledge that every person should have, but most importantly, someone who has prospects of getting into the healthcare business or making a career in the wild. The zeal that is required to learn human anatomy and work accordingly in emergencies can be very beneficial. Preparation is the key, and if you are prepared, you can win any battle in life.

15

HEADACHES, DENTAL CARE, AND MORE

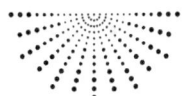

eadaches and dental issues can be termed as minor in comparison to many of the dangerous diseases, but trust me on this, these two aches can make you suffer the most! You must have felt the pain of a headache if not a toothache. Both are equally difficult on the body and the pain is somewhat excruciating.

These types of aches happen anytime without any warning or previous symptoms and can cause havoc for quite some time. The fact is that there might be numerous underlying causes of such aches. Hence, understanding the root cause of the aches has to be done thoroughly. By doing so, you will be able to understand and also at the same time will be able to cure it accordingly.

Staying out in the sun for too long, having a heated discussion, tension, worries, and even loud noises can immediately give you severe headaches. Sometimes if you drink something cold or hot and also when the weather outside is very cold, you tend to get those bad toothaches. The cause may be many, but it is a worthwhile decision to dive into what and why these aches have been troubling you.

HEADACHES

According to the World Health Organization (2019), each person in the world suffers headaches every once in a while. The severity and duration vary, as well as the underlying cause.

Types of Headaches

Let us look at the different types of headaches that there are:

- tension
- migraine
- allergy and sinus
- hormone
- hypertension
- post-traumatic
- exertion
- caffeine
- cluster

In all the different causes of headaches, two of the most common forms of headaches are chronic headaches and episodic headaches. Chronic headaches can last for days and months; this type requires serious medical attention and pain management treatment. Episodic headaches on the other hand can last thirty minutes and up to eight hours. The pain in this case comes and goes quite often.

How to Cure Headaches

- Drink water: Staying hydrated can help you with the pangs of headaches. Sometimes due to dehydration, you can feel intense pain in your head. Drink enough water every day and keep your body nourished at all times.

- Limit alcohol: Alcohol can tweak the normal function of the brain for some time, or rather while its intoxication remains. It is said that consuming alcohol can trigger migraine issues to a certain extent. Not just migraines: Alcohol can work like a diuretic, which can cause loss of fluid from the body that can eventually lead to dehydration, which again can worsen headaches.
- Use essential oils: The use of essential oils can be extremely therapeutic. Peppermint and lavender are two of the most used essential oils for headaches. Just take a few drops of the oils and rub them on your temples. It is one of the most natural and effective ways of lessening the effect of migraines.
- Apply a cold compress: If your head is burning with a headache, giving it a cold compress can help soothe the pain to a large extent. Place an ice gel or pace on the forehead and the neck regions; you will feel relieved in a matter of a few minutes.
- Drink coffee or tea: Some may find it bizarre, but it is a fact that drinking caffeinated tea can help soothe the pain of a headache. By consuming tea and coffee, the effectiveness of ibuprofen and acetaminophen increases. Ginger tea helps in soothing headaches as well.
- Try yoga: The healing properties of practicing yoga cannot be undermined. It is an effective way to release stress and can help in lessening the intensity of your headaches. According to a recent study, it has been found that practicing yoga for three months continuously resulted in a substantial decrease in the frequency of headaches (Kisan et al., 2014).
- Herbal Remedies: Certain herbal plants have the potential to soothe headaches. You can use feverfew and butterbur roots to help you cure the pain in your head (Stickler, 2020).

Many people suffer from headaches almost every moment of their lives. Headaches can cause not just severe pain, but because they can happen anytime and anywhere, they can also interfere with your plans. Imagine you are on a trip and have plans to do a lot during that period and migraine attacks frustrate you all of a sudden. Such situations are normal, and problems can happen almost any time in life. However, by using effective home remedies for your headache problems, you can soothe your head and mind to a great extent. Ensure you carry a pain relief balm and a good painkiller that can effectively give you immediate relief in no time.

TOOTHACHES

The pain that you feel when chewing or drinking something cold or hot, is called toothache. Gum irritation and infections are the topmost cause of toothaches that people suffer from. More often, the deepest reasons for a toothache can be decaying or even chipping of the tooth due to cavities. In such cases, it is recommended that you visit your dentist as soon as possible.

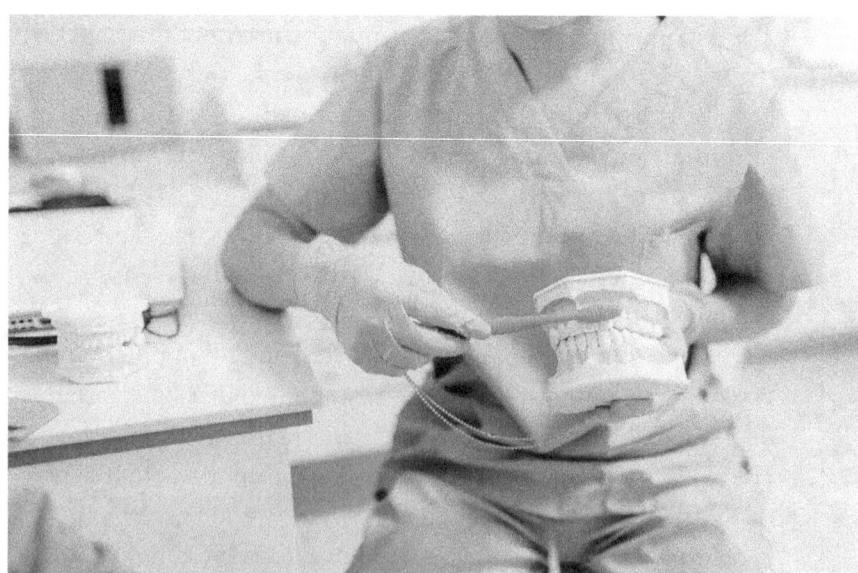

Dental care is important not just because teeth are situated at the face and can be visible; it is also important because stronger teeth can help you eat your food, which is essential to stay healthy in the long run. Additionally, neglectful teeth care can also eventually cause other health issues such as cardiovascular disease, dementia, respiratory issues, infertility, and kidney disease, to name a few ("10 Health Issues Caused by Bad Oral Health," 2021).

Toothaches Can Be Highly Painful

The nerves that are situated inside the pulp of your teeth are very sensitive. When these pulps get infected by bacteria, that can cause immense pain. Sometimes they are so sensitive that even a sip of cold coffee can generate pain that could last for days.

Causes of Toothaches

Toothaches can be caused due to several reasons. Some of these causes are as follows:

- Gum infection: Infection in the gum can cause swelling which can lead to severe pain for a very long time.
- Tooth decay: Decaying of the tooth is one of the most common reasons for toothaches. Teeth become vulnerable when they are covered with cavities and decay, causing pain now and then.
- Abscessed tooth: Bacterial infection can occur in the insides of the tooth which can result in pain and swelling of the gums.
- Tooth fracture: When the tip of the tooth chips off or gets half-broken, then that can create severe problems. The chipped tooth can sometimes hurt and cut the inner linings of the cheeks causing infection, which again can result in acute pain.

- Tooth repair: There are times when you get your tooth fixed but then later damage can occur after some time. Visit your dentist regularly and get your dental work checked.
- Rigorous chewing: Chewing on hard items can weaken the teeth from the roots. The impact of chewing continuously can be severe in terms of the health of the teeth. Something as normal as chewing a piece of gum for a long period can result in massive jaw and tooth pain.
- Eruption: Recent tooth surgery or any tooth procedure can result in swelling and pain for days. Most often dentists even recommend patients to go on a liquid diet for a few days to help heal the scars faster.

People of all ages are susceptible to problems related to teeth. Toothaches are common, and different techniques are used to heal the problem and soothe the pain for many years. Let's discuss a few methods by which you can overcome your toothaches at home.

Natural Ways to Heal Toothaches

There are many reasons that cause toothaches, but instead of jumping right in with strong medicines as a relief, you can try some of these effective home remedies (Ponsford, 2017):

- Cold compress: Most toothache problems are caused due to injured, infected gums or tooth decay. Every time you get a pain in your tooth, place an ice pack or a cold compress on top of the cheeks below the painful tooth. By applying a cold compress, you can slow down the process of blood circulation in the painful area. Apply it a couple of times and you will be able to feel the difference.
- Garlic: A compound called allicin is present in garlic which gives it medicinal value. This compound has strong antibacterial properties and can have healing effects. You

can crush the garlic with a pinch of salt and apply it directly to the affected tooth.

- Saltwater mouthwash: This is an age-old practice that most people have been following for a very long time. Take some warm water and add some salt to it, stir it well and sip and keep it in your mouth for some time. By rinsing with warm salt water, debris attached to the cavities will also get washed off and will at the same time reduce swelling of the gums. You can repeat it as many times as you need to.
- Peppermint tea: Peppermint tea has a numbing effect and when applied to the tooth, it can diffuse the pain in no time. You can use peppermint oil or prepare a solution mixed with a teaspoon of peppermint boiled in water. You can use this water to rinse your mouth occasionally.
- Clove oil: Clove oil has a numbing effect. It is readily available in the market. You can apply a drop of it on the affected tooth, but make sure to apply it with cotton and in small quantities. This is because clove oil can have a hot effect on the skin if used more.
- Aloe vera: Aloe vera gel is used mainly in conditions of cuts and burns. In recent times, people have started using it for toothaches. This is because it has antibacterial properties and can destroy germs that cause tooth decay.
- Hydrogen peroxide rinse: First of all, this solution has to be used with extra caution as it should never be swallowed. However, it has antibacterial properties because rinsing your mouth with it can help cure gum infections.
- Thyme: Thymol is a component of the essential oil that has vital antiseptic and antibiotic properties. These properties make it known for medicinal purposes. Just a drop of thyme oil in water and rinsing your mouth with it can do the trick.

Visit a Dentist

Herbal medicines and home remedies can help you get some relief from your toothache problems. Avoid eating food that has hard textures. Sugary food items can also aggravate pain. If pain and swelling last for more than a few days, then consult with your dentist immediately for treatment and regular checkups.

INSOMNIA

Insomnia is a sleep disorder that keeps you awake and even if you do manage to fall asleep, then it is only for a fleeting moment. Just the way the human body needs proper nourishment and exercise, sleep is equally important, too. Insomnia is a condition that not only disrupts your lifestyle and regular work but can also drain all your energy and make you perpetually exhausted.

The majority of adults require a minimum of seven to eight hours of sleep. Sleep issues are a common problem. Many may experience insomnia for a short-term that may last for a few days whereas some may experience insomnia that lasts for months on end. In any of the cases, insomnia can be caused due to many reasons, like traumatic experiences or some underlying health conditions.

Symptoms and Causes of Insomnia

Insomnia may result because of many problems. Some of the prominent signs and underlying reasons of insomnia are as follows ("Insomnia," 2016):

- difficulty in falling asleep
- no sound sleep
- waking up in between sleep
- waking up after a few hours
- exhausted even after sleeping
- work schedule
- excessive travel
- eating late at night
- depression, anxiety, and irritable mood swings

- feeling of sleepiness during the day
- lack of attention
- lack of focus
- caffeine and nicotine consumption
- alcohol consumption
- dull memory
- loop of worries about not having sleep

These points mentioned are all self-explanatory. If you face any of these issues, you must pay attention to where you are going wrong in your habits. Try to instill habits that will help you focus on a healthy lifestyle that can boost your sleeping habits.

There are a few other causes that could be related to the condition of insomnia ("Insomnia," 2016):

- Mental Health Disorders: Traumatic events in life can cause major sleep disorders. Feelings of anxiousness can cause severe stress and exhaustion that can adversely affect your sleeping habits.
- Medications: Some medications can cause problems in sleeping habits. Some medicines may have sedatives that could make you fall asleep, whereas some medicines contain stimulants and caffeine that could again disrupt sleep.
- Medical Conditions: Many chronic diseases have been linked with insomnia like diabetes, cancer, asthma, heart disease, overactive thyroid, Alzheimer's, and Parkinson's disease.
- Sleep-Related Disorders: Restless leg system syndrome and sleep apnea can cause major sleep disturbances.

Visit a Doctor

You can be living with insomnia for months and may be confusing it with mere feelings of anxiety or a condition of exhaustion. If you notice that your lack of proper sleep is hampering your regular life and work and is getting way beyond any control, then you must realize that it is time for you to consult with a doctor. You must understand the underlying cause of your lack of sleep. If by any chance your doctor concludes that you are suffering from a sleep disorder problem, then they will send you to a sleep center for further tests. Getting a thorough screening of your health done is beneficial. Staying focused and prepared for any situation is the best way to tackle things.

Those at Risk of Insomnia

According to the Mayo Clinic (2016), there are categories of people who are at a higher risk for insomnia:

- Over the age of 60: If you are above the age of 60, then chances are that you may be a victim of insomnia. This is because with age, sleep patterns and health conditions change and fluctuate which results in disturbance in sleep habits.
- Women: If you're a woman, then the hormonal changes that happen during the menstrual cycle and mainly during menopause, can cause severe sleep disorders. Insomnia is more common in pregnant women. The hot flashes and night sweats tend to cause disturbances in sleep.
- Mental disorder: Mental issues that result in anxiety, panic attacks, exhaustion, and frustration can all lead to a condition of loss of sleep.
- Stressed: Stress is a major factor that affects your health and most importantly, your sleep.
- Erratic schedule: Working in irregular shifts and having a messy routine can add to a habit of sleeping late that could eventually make its way toward insomnia.

Insomnia can cause tons of issues in your personal as well as your professional life. From not paying attention at work to becoming irritable and spoiling the mood of everyone around you, detrimental behavior can add up to some of the problems. With lack of sleep, you can even risk your health from acute diseases, mainly cardiovascular diseases, in the future.

Remedies That Help Insomnia

Insomnia can be controlled by instilling good sleeping habits. Here are a few ways in which you can keep your insomnia at bay ("Insomnia," 2016):

- Set a bedtime and make sure that you follow your routine of sleeping and waking up at the right time. Continue this process for a few weeks, and you will notice a vast difference in your sleep timings.
- Having an active day can help you rest well at night. Do not be a couch potato, even if it is for half an hour, make sure that you take a walk around the house or in your office area. Physical activity done during the day can help your muscles rest well at night.
- Refrain from taking naps during the day. By taking short naps in the day, you can disrupt your sleep pattern which can make you fall asleep very late at night.
- Do not eat large meals and drinks before bedtime.
- Take a warm bath before sleep and set your bed in a very comfortable way that could induce you to sleep.

Insomnia is not simply about losing your sleep, it adds to the regular functions of your life. It is not at all healthy to lose sleep, no matter what the reasons may be. Your health is in your hands, so make an effort to work your way through this problem and come out of it successfully by being insomnia-free.

CHRONIC FATIGUE

Chronic fatigue syndrome is a condition in which you experience extreme fatigue for a very long duration. Sometimes, this syndrome can last for more than six months at a time. The problem with this condition is that it cannot be cured with rest and is also tricky to diagnose.

Symptoms of Chronic Fatigue

Some of the most common signs and symptoms of chronic fatigue disorder are as follows:

- dim memory and concentration level
- sleep that does not make you feel refreshed
- dizziness when standing from a sitting posture and sitting from a lying posture

There are other symptoms that are said to be related to this condition like fatigue, sore throat, headaches, unexplained pain in the body, and enlarged lymph nodes in the armpits and neck regions.

Causes of Chronic Fatigue

Although, it is difficult to point to a particular reason for this bizarre medical condition like the chronic fatigue syndrome, here are a few potential causes that can lead to this condition ("Chronic Fatigue Syndrome," 2020):

- Viral infections: Many people get chronic fatigue syndrome after having a viral infection. Some researchers believe that a few types of viruses may be the cause of such an issue. Epstein-Barr virus and human herpes virus 6 are suspected to be the viruses involved.

- Hormonal imbalance: Hormonal imbalance has been noticed in people who have chronic fatigue syndrome. Correlations between the two have not been found, just speculation that these two issues could be related and could be causing the problem.
- Immunity problems: There is speculation whether chronic fatigue syndrome can be caused due to weak immunity. The people who suffer from this syndrome seem to have an impaired immune system.
- Emotional or physical trauma: A sudden stress or trauma could be some of the reasons for getting chronic fatigue syndrome. Many people have reported that they got this syndrome after they encountered surgery, injury, or any form of emotional trauma.

Visit a Doctor

Fatigue in general is not taken as a serious concern. A few days of rest and usually, you are good to go. However, in the case of chronic fatigue syndrome, feeling tired can last for days and months. Therefore, if you notice any of the mentioned symptoms along with a long period of unexplained fatigue, then ensure to consult with your doctor immediately.

16

BONES AND JOINTS

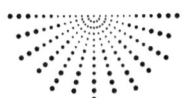

$\mathcal{B}$ones and joints have a crucial part to play in the functioning of the human body. Bones are responsible for giving strong support to the entire body. People are shaped by their bones. They support the body and safeguard vital organs such as the heart and liver.

Bones contain marrow, which produces new blood cells, and stores the minerals calcium and phosphorus. Joints, on the other hand, are the parts of the body where bones connect. They are responsible for attaching two or more bones together  so that there is a smooth function of movement.

BONE STRUCTURE

Vertebrates are the only living creatures to have bones. Due to these bones, there is some rigidity in the body. Bones play a role in storing micronutrients and also bone marrow, both essential for life.

Bone is also called an osseous tissue which is a calcified connective tissue that constitutes the endoskeleton of the human body. A matrix of ground material and collagen fibers contains osteocytes. These cells are the most prevalent type of cell in adult bone, and they are in charge of bone development and density. Calcium and phosphate are abundantly stored in the bone matrix, which further strengthens and densifies the structure. Bones are differentiated based on their shapes and placement.

Long Bones

As the name itself implies, long bones are long, and they have two ends and a shaft. Bone marrow is contained in a marrow cavity in the diaphysis or middle shaft. The epiphyses are the rounded ends of the bones that are covered in articular cartilage and packed with red bone marrow that produces blood cells. The femur, tibia, radius, and ulna are all examples of long bones that make the majority of the limb structure.

Short Bones

Short bones are also known by the name of cuboidal bones. These bones are the same length and width, which gives them a cubical shape. The ankles and wrists consist of short bones.

Flat Bones

Flat bones are slender and relatively broad bones that are present where considerable organ protection or vast muscle attachment surfaces are required. The sternum is also known as the breastbone. The scapula or shoulder blades, ribs, and the roof of the skull are all examples of flat bones.

Irregular Bones

Bones that have irregular shapes and complex nature are called irregular bones. The surfaces of these bones are short, notched, flat, or ridged. The hip bones, vertebrae, and various skull bones are examples of irregular bones.

Sesamoid Bones

Sesamoid bones are tiny in size and resemble sesame seeds in shape. The patellae are also sesamoid bones. This type of bone grows inside tendons and can be found in feet, knees, and hand joints.

Sutural Bones

Irregularly shaped bones that are small and flat in size and shape are known as sutural bones. This bone can be detected between the flat skull bones. They all vary in shape, location, and size.

JOINT INTEGRATION

The point at which two or more bones connect is called a joint. A variety of fibrous connective tissue can be found in joints. Ligaments are the connective tissues that hold the bones together. The muscles of the bones are connected by tendons. It is the cartilage that protects the end of bones by cushioning them. There are two types of joints, and they are immovable and slightly movable joints. Let's understand how they function.

Immovable and Slightly Movable Joints

In this type of joint structure, there is no presence of the joint cavity. It is the collagen and the fibrous tissues that are responsible for connecting the bones. Interestingly, the bones of the skull of an infant are flexible in the beginning, but with time, the bones join together and calcify into becoming a bone. It is the fibrous tissues that are responsible for joining the teeth in the gums. The slightly movable joints refer to the cartilaginous joints in which the bones are stuck together by cartilage as there is no joint cavity.

Synovial Joints

Synovial joints are movable joints and are very common throughout the body. Different types of synovial joints can move in different ways. Joint capsules, or fibrous tissue, surround these joints. Synovial fluid is secreted from this capsule because of the way the spaces and tissues get lubricated inside the capsule.

Ball and Socket Joints

This is a type of joint that can move and rotate in many different ways. Ball and socket joints are found in the hip and shoulder of the body.

Condyloid Joints

Condyloid joints are found in the fingers and jaw. These joints are versatile and are movable, but they cannot rotate.

Gliding Joints

These are the joints that can glide around in the body, especially in the spine, wrists, and ankles.

Hinge Joints

The parts of the human body that bends, like the knees and elbows, are composed of this type of joint.

Pivot Joints

Your neck and elbow both have pivot joints, which allow bones to pivot or twist around other bones.

Saddle Joint

The best example of this type of joint is the thumb. It can move from side to side but cannot rotate.

Range of Motion

The bones and joints in the human body are connected in such a way that some can move fully whereas some can move only partially. The degree to which a joint can move is called the range of motion. For example, the degree to which your arms connected by your elbow can move is called the range of motion.

Two different categories fall under the range of motion:

- Extension: The bones connected with the joints are placed apart and also straightened from a bent angle. Due to this, the space and angle between the joint and the bones in the limbs are increased.
- Flexion: The bones are pulled together that form the joint. In this condition, the angle and space between the joint and the bones of a limb are reduced.

CONDITIONS AFFECTING BONES AND JOINTS

There are several conditions that bones, and joints are susceptible to in terms of health-related issues.

Here are a few situations, or rather ailments, that are common:

Osteoarthritis

Arthritis is a condition that is associated with synovial joints. It is an inflammatory condition in which there is damage done to the cartilage over the years. Due to this, the cartilage thins down in the process and causes extreme pain between the bones.

Rheumatoid Arthritis

This is a condition that is associated with the immune system and its failure to save the tissues of the joints. In this autoimmune disease, the damage is done to the tissues which results in pain in the joints.

Gout

This condition is caused when the synovial joint is filled with uric acid crystals. The synovial membrane gets inflamed with use, which in turn, results in synovitis.

Fractures

Fractures are a condition when your bones get cracked or broken into a few pieces. This can be caused due to many reasons including, accident, fall, or any form of physical trauma. Although fractures are not usually a life-threatening problem, they do require an elaborate process of taking care of them. Fractures can be diagnosed with the help of an x-ray, but there are a few symptoms that could suggest a broken bone:

- excruciating pain in the injured area
- numbness in the same area
- visible swelling in the surrounding areas
- bluish color bruise
- bone protruding is seen through the skin
- heavy bleeding through the cut wound

There are different types of fractures:

- Stable: When the bone breaks but stays in its position.

- Transverse: When the fracture happens at a 90-degree angle of the bone.
- Comminuted: Most common after a trauma-like accident in which the bone gets shattered into many pieces.
- Oblique: When long bones like the femur break at an angle such that a deformity can be seen below the skin.
- Compound: Requires immediate surgery as the bone breaks and pierces through.
- Hairline: Stress fracture that happens mostly in the hands and feet due to rigorous movements like running or jogging.
- Greenstick: Only a portion of the brain breaks and also bends at the end.
- Spiral: When a bone breaks due to twisting of the limb.
- Pathological: When a patient has been ill and the bones get weakened as a result.

Fractures can happen anywhere at any time, more so, if you are out in the wild. In case you find anyone who might have a fracture, you should take the following steps immediately until the emergency team arrives:

- Stop bleeding if there is a cut or a wound.
- Apply cold in the affected area.
- Immobilize the injured person and do not allow sudden movements.
- Prepare a sling that could hold the fractured part steady and safe.
- Use the nearest available bandages and a frame of sticks to keep the hurt part upright and in place without pulling or pushing hard.
- Call the doctor immediately

Sudden accidents are bound to happen, especially when you are in the wild. If you ever face a situation where someone in your group falls and the symptoms show that they must be suffering from a fracture, then even without any medical help around, you can create a cast or a splint for the patient to keep their injury safe in a correct position. Here are a few tips on how you can go about it:

- If the arms are hurt, take a firm cloth and use it carefully to wrap it around the elbow comfortably and take the cloth upward and slowly tie it around the neck. This will immediately help immobilize the injured hand.
- For a lower leg splint, you will need padded material, preferably a foam pad that you can cut from a sleeping pad and around three cravats or anything wide enough to wrap around the splint. You can use rope to tie it around. This will give support to the legs and can help them stay in position until the medical team arrives for proper medical tests.
- Birch bark is widely used to handle a broken bone situation in the wild. The technique is simple: peel off the skin of a tree and wrap it around the affected hand or leg like you would do while making a canoe. It has natural curls which makes it easy to wrap around. You can then use any bandage at your disposal to give it support.
- Sticks and even tent poles can be used to make a temporary splint.
- If you have notebooks that have hardcovers or sleeping mats, you could use those as a material to make a splint.
- Mud casts can also be used to assist and give support to broken bones. Check a riverbank or get some wet clay and wrap it around with the help of rolled gauze in the affected area. Wrap it around the affected limbs. Slowly wrap another layer of cloth or gauze to give it support. Do not make it very heavy, just the right weight to support the bone will be enough. This will act as a plaster to keep the injured bone safe.

When taken to the emergency center, numerous tests can give a clear picture of the bone damage. From x-rays to scanning, everything will be available. Bone scanning is also done to examine the health of the bone. It is usually done to check diseases of the bone including arthritis, bone cancers, avascular necrosis, fibrous dysplasia, infection, Paget's disease, and even fractures.

Sprains

When joints like the ligaments and wrists get twisted and hurt then that is called a sprain. Your ankle can get hurt when you walk or jog and accidentally twist your foot and stretch it so hard that the ligaments which support the ankles get hurt.

Sprains are considered to be minor, but they can be divided into three categories based on the level of the damage:

- Grade 1: When the ligaments are stretched but not torn. Such sprains will be healed within a day or two. These sprains are the most common of all the sprains.
- Grade 2: When the ligament is torn partially, and the doctor can feel it when you move your ankle. Such sprains take a time of six to eight weeks to heal.
- Grade 3: When the ligament is completely torn. Such sprains take a longer time to heal, like three to six months.

Symptoms of Sprained Ankle

Here are a few symptoms to detect if you have a sprained ankle:

- bruising
- pain
- swelling
- tenderness
- instability
- restricted motion

- popping sensation

Grade 1 sprains can be treated at home. Here are a few tips on how to handle an ankle ("Home Remedies for a Sprained Ankle," 2019):

- Apply ice on the affected area.
- Apply a crepe bandage loosely and keep it on until the swelling decreases.
- Turmeric has inflammatory properties. It can be mixed with lime juice, and a few drops of water can be made into a paste to apply to the sprained area. You can apply a bandage over it.
- Garlic can also be used to treat the symptoms of a sprain. One tablespoon of crushed garlic along with some coconut oil can be applied to the affected area to reduce inflammation and pain.
- Soak the sprained ankle in warm water mixed with Epsom salt. This can have a healing effect.
- Arnica has healing properties beneficial for joints and muscles. Dilute arnica oil and gently apply it to the sprained area.
- Castor oil has pain-relieving properties and can be applied gently on the sprained portion.
- Cabbage compresses are used widely to help reduce swelling caused by a sprain.

Treating sprains can be easy and is possible without the help of a medical practitioner. It is only if the symptoms are unbearably painful that you should immediately call a doctor.

Torn Ligament

A band of fibrous tissue called ligament connects bone to bone and cartilages as well. Ligaments are not delicate but can be torn or stretched due to the sudden impact of certain joints and ankles. Sudden fall or sometimes even a high-intensity workout can lead to a ligament tear in the knees, ankles, wrists, neck, thumbs, and back.

Here are a few symptoms which indicate a case of ligament tear:

- excess pain
- tender to touch
- swelling
- bruising
- sound of pop during the time of the ligament injury

The torn ligament can be treated with ample rest, cold compress, and wrapping of crepe bandage over the affected area. Keep the ankle or the part of the body that is injured in an elevated position to control the blood circulation in that area. This will substantially reduce the swelling caused by the injury. However, if the pain persists and the swelling does not reduce after a day or two, call a doctor.

Helpful Tips

Situations can change in a minute when you are out in the wild. If you face any of the problems that we've discussed so far, it becomes imperative on your part to understand the different techniques and remedies that you could use to heal and provide the required first aid to someone who needs it the most.

Your knowledge about the human body and different illnesses can help you survive even the toughest of circumstances in the wild. From allergies to snake bites, from giving CPR to healing a wound, from making splints for an injured bone to treating various infections, you will require every bit of knowledge of medicine while you are out in the wild alone with no medical assistance nearby. The confidence that you gain through such knowledge will help you enjoy outdoor life. There will be no holding you back due to the fear of health issues. You will be prepared and will be able to handle even the most difficult situation with utmost care and calm.

17

CARING FOR OPEN WOUNDS

*O*pen wounds are always cause for concern whether you are facing them in the city or outdoors. There will be times when no matter how cautious you are while hiking or even doing a simple errand at home, you might get a cut which can result in an open wound.

Take for instance, when you're fixing your windowpane and a piece of wood breaks and slashes your arm with its sharp edge. It might happen so quickly that you may not see it coming at all. No doubt, due to the sharp edge, you will get a cut. Cuts, if left open, can cause severe hazards: you can bleed profusely, and at the same time, can get severe infections.

Similarly, in a rather difficult situation in the wilderness while hiking, if you get a severe cut, leaving it open can cause acute health hazards. It is profoundly important to deal with open wounds because these kinds of wounds are common. By gaining knowledge about how to prepare for a situation with open wounds, you can help prevent dangerous infections.

WHAT IS AN OPEN WOUND?

An open wound, as the name suggests, refers to an accident that has caused the internal and external body tissues to break. This type of wound is generally located near the skin area. From childhood to becoming an adult, almost everyone is bound to experience this type of wound sometime in their lives.

Most open wounds are treatable at home, but again, the depth and the size of the cut matter. Many times, when the cut is too deep, stitches will be required which can be provided by an experienced professional only. In such a case, it is best to visit the doctor as soon as possible. The treatment of open wounds depends on the type of the wound.

TYPES OF OPEN WOUNDS

Abrasion

When your body rubs against a coarse surface and gets scraped then that is called abrasion. You must have noticed when you fall or even during bike accidents, people get abrasions on their arms, hands, knees, limbs, and faces. Abrasions affect the outer layer of skin, therefore, there is no case of intense bleeding. Most of the time, such abrasions are cleaned with an antiseptic wash and then an ointment is applied. It needs to be lightly bandaged to avoid any external infection. In no time, such abrasions dry off and heal completely.

Puncture

When you get hit by a pointy object, it causes a puncture through the skin. When a person gets hit by a bullet, that also forms a puncture. The wound that is formed by a puncture can be very deep, harming internal organs. However, not much bleeding happens with minor punctures.

For wounds like this, you need to visit a medical practitioner and get tests done to see if there is any internal bleeding.

Laceration

Open wounds are caused by sharp objects like knives, machinery, and tools with sharp edges. This kind of cut can cause rapid and heavy bleeding. Therefore, the primary step to help is to make an effort to stop the bleeding immediately.

Avulsion

These are wounds caused due to violent accidents and explosions. Tearing of the skin and tissue makes this wound a painful one. The bleeding through such a wound can be very heavy, and you must immediately try and stop the bleeding of the person suffering from it.

TREATMENT OF OPEN WOUNDS

There is a wide range of treatments available for open wounds. The treatments depend on the type and depth of the wound. Some minor open wounds can be easily treated at home or anywhere outside.

However, wounds that are severe and which have a chance of getting a bad infection, must be treated immediately.

Home Remedies to Treat Open Wounds

Wounds have to be immediately washed off with a disinfectant liquid or any soap available. This will help clean the wound and prevent infections from spreading further. After you clean the wound from all the dirt and debris, make sure you place direct pressure on the opening to stop any bleeding.

Use an antibacterial or antibiotic ointment or gel and apply it gently over the injury. Place a light bandage over the top to keep it clean. Very small wounds do not require any bandaging.

There will be pain and some swelling; if they are mild, then you just need some good rest. For the pain, you can take a mild painkiller. Ensure that you avoid medicines like aspirin, as that can encourage more bleeding.

For the selling, you can use a cold compress of ice. If you are out in the woods, you will have to follow the same procedures, but one thing you could add is to apply a light layer of sunscreen on the area of injury to protect it from the harsh heat until it heals completely.

Know When to Call For Help

Minor wounds can be controlled and taken care of; what matters is when to realize that the wound is major. This is not a problem if you are near the reach of a health facility in the city but can be a huge problem if you are out in the wilderness.

Cuts and abrasions are common when you are on an expedition in the outdoors, but for wounds that are deep and acute, it is best to evacuate your position and head toward the nearest health center.

Here are a few reasons that should make you realize that it is time for evacuation from the outdoors:

- If the wound is big and needs sutures or stitches.
- If the wound contains debris that has seeped in it during the accident.
- If the wound has been caused by an animal attack. Animal paws and teeth can cause fatal infections.
- If there are symptoms like chills, fever, excessive swelling, and red bruises.
- If the wound is wide enough to expose the bones, especially the joints.
- If the cut is very deep and is on the face.
- If the wound has coverage of dead tissues around.
- If the bleeding does not stop even after trying all the first aid methods.
- If the wound is preventing any mobility.

If you are in the wild, one of the disadvantages that you face is the lack of proper cellular coverage. In times like this, it will be impossible for you to call anyone for help. One of the cautionary measures that you can take before setting on a trip in the wild is carrying two or three simple phones that have different network providers. Switch them off while you do not need them, but you can check if any of the networks can get a call through when the situation arises.

Stab Wound

Globally, the crime rate seems to be increasing by the day. There are numerous miscreants out there, of whom you can never be aware. Due to such reasons, sometimes traveling alone, and especially taking long expeditions by yourself, can be a bit risky. This thought, though, should not stop you from taking the trip that you've always wanted to or your desire to seek the wilderness. The point is that you must always be prepared to be safe and also should be aware of some of the most essential self-defense techniques

When you venture out in the wild, you must have a strong heart to face challenges and deal with the problems if there are any. For instance, you are on your way to mountainous terrain, and your car is approached by a person who has been stabbed and thrown on the road. Of course, your first step must be to immediately call the cops and ambulance. But while you wait for the help to arrive, you can do your bit to help the person survive.

It is evident that since you are on your journey to the outdoors, you will have your first aid kit with you. Here are a few ways to help a stabbed person:

- When you encounter a stabbed person, your primary concern will be to stop the bleeding. Never forget to wear your gloves before touching anything that has an opening or blood in it. Do not wash the injury because it is a major one, it will be given a thorough cleaning at the hospital.

- Make the person lie or sit in a comfortable position to avoid dizziness or fainting.
- Check if there is anything external stuck in the injury. If you find something in, do not attempt to remove it.
- Try to elevate the part that is injured above the heart to slow down the bleeding to some extent.
- Most important of all, apply direct pressure on the wound to stop heavy bleeding.
- Talk gently to the patient and make an effort to maintain the patient's full consciousness.

By taking care of the stabbed patient until the medical rescue team reaches the scene, can help them survive.

How to Close Wounds

Major wounds must always be treated at a hospital. However, if you do not find a way to reach any medical help soon, then closing a wound should be one of the last options.

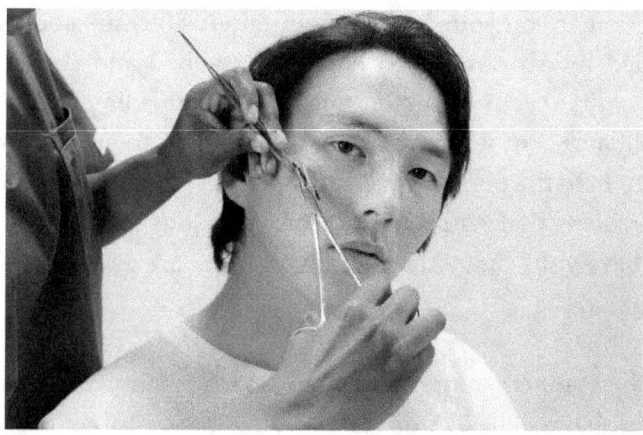

There are many different ways in which wounds can be closed and some of them are listed below

Staples

Surgical staples are considered to be a reasonable method to help close an open wound. This method can be used when there is no time to take the patient to a proper medical center on time. You can use staples quite quickly and this can be highly helpful in controlling bleeding. In cases of multiple wounds, this technique can be fast and efficient. Using surgical staples needs minimal training and can be highly cost-effective as well. If done correctly and hygienically, the healing time of this method is the same as sutures. Always ensure that the staple that you use is thoroughly sanitized to prevent any form of infection in the process.

Sutures

Sutures are a common and very old conventional method to seal a wound. Sutures are of two different types, absorbable and non-absorbable. Absorbable sutures are strong enough that the chemicals of the body will not be able to dissolve them. These sutures are mostly used in external wounds and cuts. However, for surgeries that require double layer closing, like in the case of uterus surgery, then absorbable sutures will work the best as there will be no requirement to open the sutures again. The choice of sutures that should be used completely depends on the nature of the wound.

In the case of long wounds, a running suture is said to be the most beneficial. For a deep wound, a mattress stitch can also be used as it is said to give stronger support to the wound.

Adhesives

Skin adhesive is the easiest and painless option that can be used to close an open wound. You can firmly but with a gentle hand, carefully place the adhesive on the cut and bring the skin together slowly and stick it with adhesive. Using adhesive narrows down your chance of getting an infection way more than sutures. The use of adhesives is the best option for a person who is out in the wild. However, here are a few things that you need to be cautious about while dealing with open wounds:

- Clean the area thoroughly before applying any form of suture or adhesive.
- Place the edges of the skin gently with each other and then apply the adhesive over it.
- Refrain from pulling the skin very hard to bring them closer. This can cause the wound to tear more.
- Finally, when the position is set correctly, use a skin adhesive or glue to seal the wound.

Be aware of the hygiene process and never touch a wound with anything dirty. Always carry an antiseptic wash and a cream with you. They are handy and can be used in many ways.

Healing Process

After the treatment of open wounds, the healing process can take a while and may be different for every individual. Many factors can slow down the process of healing. Ensure that you monitor the wound and give the appropriate dressing on time.

Factors like oxygen not reaching the wound through proper blood circulation can be one of the reasons why a wound may heal slowly. Such wounds can take double the time compared to a wound that receives adequate oxygen and nutrient supply through the blood. High blood sugar levels, blood pressure, and even obesity can slow down the process of healing.

Wound dressing is the key to clearing out a wound. Ensure you do it regularly by maintaining all the hygiene protocols; in just a matter of days, the wound will start drying up and eventually heal completely. Observe your patient for some time, and if the wound has developed an infection and is not healing fast enough, then make sure that you consult the doctor immediately.

18

TENDING TO THE PATIENT

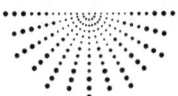

When a patient goes through any trauma or sickness, there is a high probability that they will not behave the same as they would in normal circumstances. People are different, and it is their personal, mental, and physical capacity that can help them deal with a situation. As a medical asset, it is a requirement that you should know all the basics of medicine and treatment. However, the most challenging part of your job will be to deal with a panicky patient in a time of crisis.

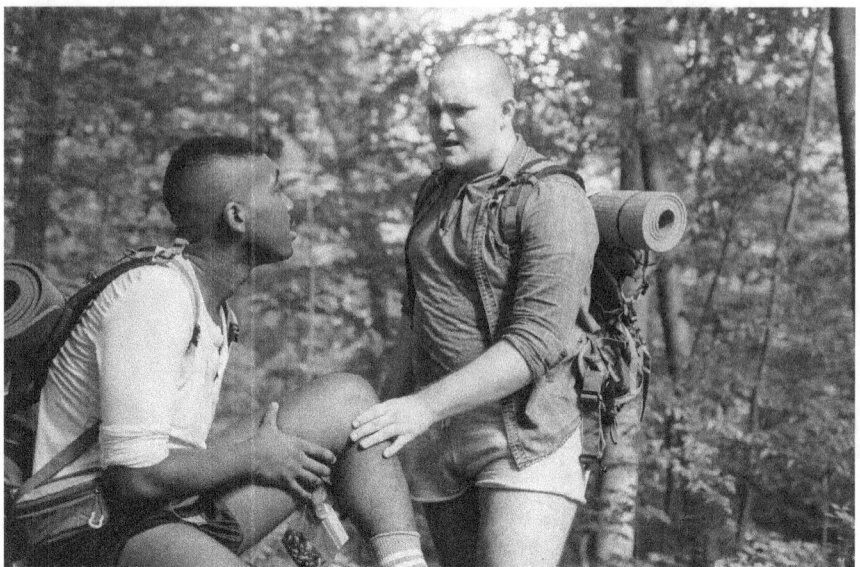

The comfort and ease of mind that a patient needs is something that as a healthcare person you must understand. The psychology of patients can range per patient and can be difficult to decode. With years of experience and most importantly with an urge to understand the situation, you will be able to help patients when they need your support the most.

HOW TO CALM YOUR PATIENT

Different patients will have different personalities, and it is up to you to figure out how to deal with each one of them. Sometimes the pain and the trauma caused by the illness or even accidents, for that matter, may cause disillusionment and can also give them a panic attack. In such a situation, you as their medical person can follow a few simple methods to help them calm down.

Be Engaging

As soon as the patient arrives or you meet the patient, engage them by asking them simple questions. Listen to them with attention and make them feel that they are heard. This can naturally calm down an anxious patient.

Give Relevant Information

While checking on the patient, you can talk and give relevant information about what the treatment will be like and how you plan to go ahead with it. Keeping them engaged in the process can help them think clearly. Ensure that the flow of communication between you and the patient is easy and without any confusion, as even a slight point of misunderstanding can cause panic and anxiety. Patience will be the key in dealing with patients who often experience some form of trauma or shock.

If you work for an organization, be aware of any policies or clauses that may prevent you from indulging and disclosing specific information to your patients. You must always be careful of what extra, unnecessary information you might indulge in giving. While doing so, inquire about the patient's medical history. Do not coerce the patients; instead, give them ample time to answer your questions.

Do Not Complicate Things

Keep things simple by speaking to the patient rather than using medical jargon. By asking simple inquiries about how they feel and other health-related questions, you can divert your patient's thoughts from a state of anxiety, to one of stability. Your objective should be clear, and in any medical situation, it should be to make the patient feel better. Think with clarity while dealing with a case and take one step at a time. Examine every symptom and indicator before jumping to any conclusions. Utilize your expertise gained through experience, investigate all aspects of the situation, and then come to a decision to assist in the treatment of the issues.

Address Their Worries

Addressing their worries by asking them what they are fearing can help an anxious patient talk about their problems. By understanding their thoughts, you can give them sound advice and help them with their concerns. The most crucial skill is being a good listener. As a medical professional, you must always be aware of your patient's state of mind before beginning a treatment procedure. It is a natural process that when you address people's fears and conditions, you will be able to understand the situation and, as a result, it will be easier for you to solve the issue and keep the patient safe. More attention should be paid to what they are concerned about, and then a treatment plan should be devised accordingly.

Stay Calm

An anxious patient can have a panic attack if they realize that the medical practitioner is stressed. No matter how difficult you may find the situation and how complicated the case may look, ensure that in front of the patient, you do not lose your cool. Stay calm and make the patient realize that you are in a good mood. The confidence that you ooze out of your personality is what will help your patients feel safe and a sense of calm.

The self-assurance that you exude from your personality is what will make your patients feel secure and at ease. It's unusual for patients to function effectively in a confined, distracting environment. Having a calm approach to interacting with your patients can aid you in comprehending even the most difficult situations. Panic and hostility will not help you in a difficult situation. As a result, you must understand that by being calm, you will be able to treat your patients in a much better way.

Lighten Their Mood

If you find the patient is extremely tense, then you can ask them light questions that can help divert their mind to something else. Ask them about their hobbies and what they like to eat, etc. By creating such distractions, you can engage your patient even when they are in panic mode.

Empathize

Tell your patient that what they are feeling is normal. Ask them to stay calm as that can help them get better soon.

Patients who feel that they are taken care of well seem to be much calmer during any medical procedures. Such an attitude can be a huge determining factor in how a person will recover during and after a treatment process.

Every case will be different in terms of the patient's behavior and receptive capability. You can use the following measures to find more information:

- Consider co-occurring disorders: While you attend to the patient analyze the situation and think if there could be anything they are not telling you. Ask questions gently and try to get as much information as you can.
- Immediately start considering any doubts that you feel regarding their present situation. If you have any concerns about the cause of the problem, make sure to note them down.
- Be mindful of situations that can take place later during or after the treatment and make arrangements to have a smooth treatment process.
- Take their overall mental health into account: It is always wise to understand the mental health of a patient. Many times, patients tend to give a wrong narration of their injury or illness, and at times they can exaggerate situations. This can affect and have serious consequences on the treatment that you will provide. Be sure that what the patient is saying is correct, try to understand the state of mind of the patient by asking a few cross-questions, and then go ahead with the treatment accordingly.

- Medical history: Medical history is important and many people, unknowingly, fear talking about the medical issues they've had in the past. Figure out ways to ask them if they've had any particular medicine or previous symptoms. Be tricky but in a very subtle manner and get information on their health.
- Ask if they are taking any medication or under treatment for any other disease. This is because some medicines cannot be given at the same time and can cause serious reactions. Their present physical and mental health should be open to you before you start on your procedure to treat the patient. Every person responds to the same medication in different ways, be sure of what treatment you plan to give them and how they can deal with it.

ALLERGIES

Sometimes conditions that may look very serious may be a result of allergies that even the patients may not be aware of having. Understanding allergies in such a case can be very useful.

If you are in the wild, then your chances of encountering allergic reactions may be many.

With the following information, you will be able to sail yourself through even in the toughest of allergic problems:

- Find out what you are allergic to. By identifying the root cause of your allergy, you can protect yourself and at the same time, can fight it more effectively. Some people are allergic to dust, pollen, grasses, weeds, certain plants, trees, oils, food, and even fruit.
- Develop a plan to protect yourself from allergies. If you get highly affected by pollen grains, then make sure you avoid outdoors during spring when there is a huge rush of pollen grains being transported by bees and other insects. Keep your windows and doors at your home shut.
- Avoid eating food items that have an adverse reaction in your body.
- Clean yourself thoroughly to avoid any external dirt or allergic component attacking your system.
- Wear a mask if you have dust and pollen allergies.
- Inhalation treatment through steam can also be done to clean your nose pipes where allergens can be hidden.

- Try alternative methods to heal your allergy problems like acupuncture and other natural herbal remedies.

To counter allergies, you must be sure of your triggers. Once you're sure of what makes you sick, half your battle is already won. You can avoid whatever makes you allergic and stay safe in the long run.

DEALING WITH STINGS, BITES, AND ALL THINGS BUGS

The ecosystem is abundant with a wide range of insects and bugs. If you love the wild and are a regular wilderness explorer, then you must know by now that stings and bites can be some of the most common problems while out on an expedition.

In the US and surrounding regions, ticks, wasps, mosquitoes, bees, and even spiders and scorpions can be found in abundance. Every bite of these creatures is different and has a different result. Some just cause irritation whereas some are capable of spreading venom in the body.

It will be a wise decision to venture out in the wild with a few options in mind for dealing with such issues:

- Always carry a strong insect repellent.
- Choose a safe spot potentially free of harmful insects especially for a halt or a night stay.
- If a bee stings, then immediately remove the stinger. Use a tweezer for the process.
- Clean a bite or a sting area in the skin immediately with soap and water.
- Do not scratch the affected areas.
- Never go near a bee, hornet, or a wasp's nest. Keep in mind that some types of bees and wasps make nests in the ground.
- A cold compress or an ice pack will always help in such a situation. It can even help reduce swelling.

- For serious allergic reactions, make sure you carry your antiallergic medicine and shots.
- If the allergic reaction does not soothe even after an anti-allergic shot, then rush the patient to the nearest healthcare facility.

When you are on a hike in the outdoors, the chances are high that many insects like ticks and spiders can clutch in your clothes, and you may not even realize. Do not sleep with the clothes that you've traveled in through the woods. If changing is not possible, then dust your entire body with a piece of cloth.

Spider and scorpion stings can be fatal at times. When you encounter such a situation, first wash the affected area with antiseptic soap and water and then apply a cold compress. Observe if there are any symptoms like muscle spasm, nausea, vomiting, convulsions, and impaired speech and if so, do not wait any longer, rush the patient to the nearest medical center immediately.

SKIN ISSUES

Skin issues can be another problem while out in the woods. Refrain from touching plants that you've not been in contact with before. There are numerous plants out in the woods that can cause serious rashes and allergies to the skin.

Not just plants and insects, overexposure to the sun or the snow can cause the skin to burn. Always use a sunscreen lotion on your exposed skin even if there is no visible sun.

Carry anti-allergic medicines and skin-soothing creams that can cool your rashes and provide you relief from the constant itches and pain.

Cover your face with a light scarf while you are moving around the forest areas.

TRANSPORTING THE PATIENT

If you encounter any patient in the wild who has fallen from a cliff or just had a bad accident in the woods, do not move their body instantly. Injuries are not always visible and can be internal as well. It is your duty as a medical person to keep the patient as safe as possible in any given situation.

The first thought that will always come to your mind is to shift the patient to a stable and comfortable place for further treatment. Here are a few techniques that you can use to lift and safely move the patient:

- drags
- basic drag
- blanket drag
- backpack carry
- chair carry
- fireman's carry
- four-hand seat
- improvised harness carry
- papoose sling
- piggyback
- supported piggyback
- two-person carry
- wheelbarrow carry
- improvised litters

Apart from these techniques, you can use blankets and thick clothes to carry the patient by four people like a stretcher. Woods and long bamboo plants can be tied with each other to make stretchers. In the wild where there are no medical accessories available, if you have to rush the patient from a hill to the medical center, then you can use some of these methods to smoothly carry them without causing any further damage to their injury. Ensure that the patient is not jerked, pulled, or pushed during the process.

SERVING AS A NURSE

When you've made a decision and commitment to become a medical asset, you must always be mindful that emergencies can crop up at any time and can happen to anyone. Once you've taken up the role as a caregiver, it is your prerogative to be available for those in need around you.

There might be situations where you might be caught up with other priorities of your own, in such cases, make sure that you direct the patient to another trusted caregiver.

PROPER USE OF ANTIBIOTICS

Antibiotics have been mentioned a couple of times in this book and rightly so, as any survival kit will have its share of antibiotics. Antibiotics should be used as per a doctor's consultation and even if you decide to use them at your discretion, then listed below are a few dos and don'ts for the usage of antibiotics.

Dos

- Use antibiotics smartly and with caution.
- Consume them in correct doses and for the exact time period only. Do not stop taking them as soon as you feel better; finish the course as prescribed or directed.
- Consume only if needed.
- Antibiotics treat bacteria caused infections like whooping cough, strep throat, and urinary tract infections.

Don'ts

- Do not consume antibiotics regularly.
- Antibiotics do not work on cold symptoms, sore throats, flu, and bronchitis.
- Antibiotics are not needed for sinus infections.

Make sure that you take antibiotics exactly as prescribed by your doctor. Do not self-medicate as that can cause more complications later on. Some side effects like rash, nausea, yeast infections, and diarrhea can be caused due to the usage of antibiotics. Make sure that you immediately call the doctor if the symptoms persist.

EMERGENCY CHILDBIRTH

Pregnancy and childbirth can be tricky situations if you are in the backcountry. Dealing with pregnancy is way easier than having to deal with delivering a sudden child out in the open. If you are trained and have knowledge about pregnancy-related concerns and childbirth, then you can very well save lives in an emergency. Here are some of the most important steps that you must take when you encounter a woman in labor:

- Immediately call 911 or any local emergency number.
- If you notice the pregnant woman's water is broken, and there is time for the medics to arrive, then lay her down in a comfortable place.
- Labor contractions can be long or short depending on the woman.
- If the woman says that she is getting cramps, then start preparing for the delivery process.
- Observe if the labor pressure is getting faster; faster means that the child is approaching.
- Maintain your cool and try to calm the woman by making her take long breaths.
- As the woman approaches the transitional phase, she will start making an effort to push naturally.
- Look into her vagina and check if the baby's head can be seen. Encourage her to take long breaths and to keep pushing.

- Ensure you support the head of the baby as it begins to come out. Once the head is out, the rest of the baby's body will easily follow.
- Be extra careful as the newborn will be slippery.
- As soon as the baby cries, keep the baby on the mother's chest and keep the child covered with something warm.
- The final and the most crucial step is to deal with the placenta. This is a vital part, as the placenta will take from 10 minutes to an hour to come out of the mother's body. With a little bit of pressure, the mother will push the placenta out.
- Firmly but with extra caution, massage her body slowly, making sure the bleeding stops.

Delivering a baby can be a difficult task, and it is advised not to practice this if you have no proper medical training. However, at times during emergencies, knowing about childbirth can help you in humongous ways.

Knowledge about various medical conditions can turn into a blessing if you can save someone's life. How you deal with an injured person or a person who is ill cannot just help you gain experience but can make you realize the importance of learning the knowledge of medicine.

Leave a 1-Click Review!

Customer reviews

 5 out of 5

3 global ratings

5 star		100%
4 star		0%
3 star		0%
2 star		0%
1 star		0%

˅ How are ratings calculated?

Review this product

Share your thoughts with other customers

Write a customer review

AFTERWORD

In a fast moving world like this, being a medical asset can make you highly relevant. It is a job that cannot just give you a good payoff but can be equally rewarding as well. The confidence that you can gain by becoming adept in knowing and understanding various concepts of medicine, from acupuncture and traditional medicines to herbal treatments, from survival strategies in the wild to basic medical knowledge including childbirth, can help you evolve in unimaginable ways.

Your pursuit of medical education can help you have a successful prospect, making you useful in every place that you go. Whether you plan to work continuously as a medical practitioner or you want to venture out in the wild for a little longer, one thing that remains constant is the knowledge that can help you save your life as well as those around you.

Preparation is always good. You do not have to worry about preparing because something negative might happen. If that is your perspective, then that can attract a more negative vibe around you. Keep your focus on what you want and learn to face any difficulty. The goal is to become so competent, that even the most challenging times will crumble in the light of your knowledge.

There can be no virtue better than that of saving another's life. It is not just a job; the point remains that you are capable of saving people. Use your knowledge in the best possible way, and the contentment that you receive will be beyond any comparison.

Therefore, grab that first aid bag and begin your journey of becoming a medical asset. Think of all the lives that you will be able to save and the journeys that you can take in the wilderness without any fear. Your knowledge will become your confidence. No age is too young or too old to start a new journey or to gain a new education. Take a step forward, and the road ahead will all be yours!

REFERENCES

All images sourced from Unsplash

https://unsplash.com/photos/NVyRLLQutd8

https://unsplash.com/photos/XDPjmeRj7bQ

https://unsplash.com/photos/L3hyEbDk194

https://unsplash.com/photos/JQ7Ng6OgzDM

https://unsplash.com/photos/siD6uufCyt8

https://unsplash.com/photos/kab6rZITjaI

https://unsplash.com/photos/2XZ-tIRRt04

https://unsplash.com/photos/TZw891-oMio

https://unsplash.com/photos/Zjyx5CYVcho

https://unsplash.com/photos/EenUxvVltMs

https://unsplash.com/photos/hcxqLJjI99E

https://unsplash.com/photos/JkGq84BiHm0

https://unsplash.com/photos/-fP2-cL-6_U

Accidental Hippies. (2017, November 23). *9 Tips for Planning The Perfect Homestead Layout*. Accidental Hippies. https://www.accidental-hippies.com/2017/11/23/perfect-homestead-layout/

Allanwood, G. (2018). Dash the Rabbit. In *Unsplash*. https://unsplash.com/photos/hcxqLJjI99E

Amabile, T. M., & Kramer, S. J. (2016, June 8). *The Power of Small*

Wins. Harvard Business Review. https://hbr.org/2011/05/the-power-of-small-wins

Animated Spirit. (2018, March 5). *A Farmer's Mindset*. Animated Spirit. http://www.animatedspirit.com/a-farmers-mindset/

Berman, M. G., Jonides, J., & Kaplan, S. (2008). The Cognitive Benefits of Interacting With Nature. *Psychological Science, 19*(12), 1207–1212. https://doi.org/10.1111/j.1467-9280.2008.02225.x

Berto, R. (2005). Exposure to restorative environments helps restore attentional capacity. *Journal of Environmental Psychology, 25*(3), 249–259. https://doi.org/10.1016/j.jenvp.2005.07.001

Boeckmann, C. (2021a, January 6). *Starting Seeds Indoors: How and When to Start Seeds*. Old Farmer's Almanac. https://www.almanac.com/starting-seeds-indoors-how-and-when-start-seeds

Boeckmann, C. (2021b, March 25). *Vegetable Gardening for Beginners*. Old Farmer's Almanac. https://www.almanac.com/vegetable-gardening-for-beginners

Boeckmann, C. (2021a, June 3). *Companion Planting Guide for Vegetables*. Old Farmer's Almanac. https://www.almanac.com/companion-planting-chart-vegetables

Boeckmann, C. (2021b, July 2). *How to Pickle*. Old Farmer's Almanac. https://www.almanac.com/how-to-pickle

Caden, K. (2020). Easy DIY Chicken Coop Plans. In *Organic Consumers*. https://www.organicconsumers.org/sites/default/files/chickencoop-buildplans.com_free_5_chicken_barn_plans.pdf

Cagle, B. (2015). Arkansas Chickens. In *Unsplash*. https://unsplash.com/photos/EenUxvVltMs

Carlson, R. (2017). *Food Preservation Methods | Which One Is Right For You?* Homesteading.com. https://homesteading.com/food-preservation-methods/

Common Sense Home. (2017, February 14). *7 Best Chicken Tips for First Time Chicken Owners*. Common Sense Home. https://commonsensehome.com/best-chicken-tips/

Dana. (2018, December 19). *The 5 Best Farm Animals for Beginners to*

Raise. Fantail Valley Homestead. https://piwakawakavalley.-co.nz/best-farm-animals-beginners/

Deep Green Permaculture. (2013, October 1). *No Dig Gardening, Sustainable Gardening With Less Effort.* Deep Green Permaculture. https://deepgreenpermaculture.com/diy-instructions/no-dig-gardening/

Deep Green Permaculture. (2016, April 3). *Wicking Bed Construction, How to Build a Self-Watering Wicking Bed.* Deep Green Permaculture. https://deepgreenpermaculture.com/diy-instructions/wicking-bed-construction/

Earth Friendly Tips. (2020a, April 29). *How to Start a Garden for Beginners.* Earth Friendly Tips. https://earthfriendlytips.com/how-to-start-a-garden-for-beginners/

Earth Friendly Tips. (2020b, May 27). *Best Plants for Beginner Gardeners.* Earth Friendly Tips. https://earthfriendlytips.com/best-plants-for-beginner-gardeners/

Eartheasy. (2021a). *A Beginner's Guide to Dehydrating Food.* Eartheasy Guides & Articles. https://learn.eartheasy.com/guides/a-beginners-guide-to-dehydrating-food/

Eartheasy. (2021b). *Natural Garden Pest Control.* Eartheasy Guides & Articles. https://learn.eartheasy.com/guides/natural-garden-pest-control/

EcoScraps. (2021). *EcoScraps - Planting By Zone: A Complete Guide.* Www.ecoscraps.com. https://www.ecoscraps.com/blogs/gardening-farming/87136132-planting-by-zone-a-complete-guide

Elena. (2016). *Blog - DIY Well Digging- How to Drive Your Own Well.* Www.thereadystore.com. https://www.thereadystore.com/blog/diy-well-digging-how-to-drive-your-own-well

Farm Health Online. (2018). *Farm Health Online – Animal Health and Welfare Knowledge Hub – Environment.* Farm Health Online. https://www.farmhealthonline.com/US/health-welfare/cattle/environment/

Forestry Commission. (2015, June 18). *What is coppicing?* Www.youtube.com. https://www.youtube.com/watch?v=FkRuMqVu-JDE&t=128s&ab_channel=ForestryCommission

Gardener, A. (2018, July 16). How to Build a Chicken Wire Fence | Blain's Farm & Fleet Blog. *Blain's Farm & Fleet Blog*. https://www.farmandfleet.com/blog/build-chicken-wire-fence/

Gardening Channel. (2020, September 14). *How to Design and Build Your Greenhouse Plans*. Gardening Channel. https://www.gardeningchannel.com/greenhouse-plan-designs/

Garone, S. (2021, June 30). *Is Homeschooling Right for Your Family?* Verywell Family. https://www.verywellfamily.com/the-pros-and-cons-of-homeschooling-5074888

Gilmour. (2019, April 4). *Planting Zones Map - Find Your Plant Hardiness Growing Zone*. Gilmour. https://gilmour.com/planting-zones-hardiness-map

Goat Farmers. (2019). *9-Step Essential Beginners Guide to Raising Goats*. Goatfarmers.com. https://www.goatfarmers.com/blog/beginners-guide-raising-goats%2F

Grace, A. (2020). Garden Stone Pathway with Greenery and Flowers. In *Unsplash*. https://unsplash.com/photos/L3hyEbDk194

Growing With Nature. (2019, April 1). *What You Need to Know About Permaculture Zones*. Growing with Nature. https://www.growingwithnature.org/permaculture-zones/

Harvard Health Publishing. (2010, July). *Spending time outdoors is good for you, from the Harvard Health Letter - Harvard Health*. Harvard Health; Harvard Health. https://www.health.harvard.edu/press_releases/spending-time-outdoors-is-good-for-you

Hicks Nurseries. (2019, March 11). *When And How To Prune Plants | Pruning With A Purpose*. Hicks Nurseries. https://hicksnurseries.com/trees-and-shrubs/pruning-plants-purpose/

Homeschool Legal Defense Association. (2021). *Homeschool Laws By State*. HSLDA. https://hslda.org/legal

Homesteading Family. (2020, May 9). *HOW TO MAKE A DIY BEAN TUNNEL (OR HOOP HOUSE)*. Www.youtube.com. https://www.youtube.com/watch?v=ilosaVqiSlc

Hosfeld, D. (2019, October 2). *Off Grid Electricity: What You Need to Know*. An off Grid Life. https://www.anoffgridlife.com/off-grid-electricity-what-you-need-to-know/

Jacobs, J. M., Cohen, A., Hammerman-Rozenberg, R., Azoulay, D., Maaravi, Y., & Stessman, J. (2008). Going Outdoors Daily Predicts Long-Term Functional and Health Benefits Among Ambulatory Older People. *Journal of Aging and Health, 20*(3), 259–272. https://doi.org/10.1177/0898264308315427

Jacobs, R. (2020). Organic Fruit fresh Farmer's Market. In *Unsplash*. https://unsplash.com/photos/JkGq84BiHm0

Jefferies, S. (2021, May 27). *Living Off the Grid: Can You Afford the Costs?* GOBankingRates. https://www.gobankingrates.com/saving-money/budgeting/living-off-the-grid/

Kaplan, S. (1995). The restorative benefits of nature: Toward an integrative framework. *Journal of Environmental Psychology, 15*(3), 169–182. https://doi.org/10.1016/0272-4944(95)90001-2

Kendra. (2010, February 23). *Building A Survival Food Storage On The Homestead • New Life On A Homestead*. New Life on a Homestead. https://www.newlifeonahomestead.com/building-our-food-storage/

Lewis, J. (2020). Homeschooling. In *Unsplash*. https://unsplash.com/photos/-fP2-cL-6_U

Li, Q., Morimoto, K., Kobayashi, M., Inagaki, H., Katsumata, M., Hirata, Y., Hirata, K., Shimizu, T., Li, Y. J., Wakayama, Y., Kawada, T., Ohira, T., Takayama, N., Kagawa, T., & Miyazaki, Y. (2008). A forest bathing trip increases human natural killer activity and expression of anti-cancer proteins in female subjects. *Journal of Biological Regulators and Homeostatic Agents, 22*(1), 45–55. https://pubmed.ncbi.nlm.nih.gov/18394317/

Lins, E. (2021). Small House in Wintertime and Pathways. In *Unsplash*. https://unsplash.com/photos/NVyRLLQutd8

Lippl, F. J., Neubauer, S., Schipfer, S., Lichter, N., Tufman, A., Otto, B., & Fischer, R. (2010). Hypobaric Hypoxia Causes Body Weight Reduction in Obese Subjects. *Obesity, 18*(4), 675–681. https://doi.org/10.1038/oby.2009.509

M, R. (2016, February 8). *How To Find The Best Place To Drill Your Own Well*. Off the Grid News. https://www.offthegridnews.com/how-to-2/how-to-find-the-best-place-to-dig-your-own-well/

Magyar, C. (2019, November 27). *35 Ways to Make Money From*

Your Homestead - A Comprehensive Guide. Rural Sprout. https://www.ruralsprout.com/make-money-from-your-homestead/

MasterClass. (2020, November 8). *Guide to Planting Zones: What to Grow in 13 Hardiness Zones.* MasterClass. https://www.masterclass.com/articles/guide-to-planting-zones#how-to-use-hardiness-zones-when-planting-a-garden

Mazzoni, M. (2020, January 21). *Are Wood Pallets Safe for Reuse Projects? It Depends.* Earth911. https://earth911.com/health/how-to-safely-use-pallet-wood/

Morin, A. (2014, November 23). *7 Scientifically Proven Benefits Of Gratitude That Will Motivate You To Give Thanks Year-Round.* Forbes. https://www.forbes.com/sites/amymorin/2014/11/23/7-scientifically-proven-benefits-of-gratitude-that-will-motivate-you-to-give-thanks-year-round/?sh=3d299954183c

Ohio State University. (2016, September 30). *Food Preservation: Freezing Basics.* Ohioline.osu.edu. https://ohioline.osu.edu/factsheet/hyg-5341

Oregon State University Ecampus. (2016, May 2). *Permaculture Zones.* Www.youtube.com. https://youtu.be/CaUlnvGhnho

Permaculture Apprentice. (2018, May 16). *How to Set up a Permaculture Farm in 9 Steps - Permaculture Apprentice.* Permaculture Apprentice. https://permacultureapprentice.com/how-to-set-up-a-permaculture-farm/

Permaculture Apprentice. (2020, May 9). *How to choose the best location for your crisis garden (site assessment guide).* Permaculture Apprentice. https://permacultureapprentice.com/crisis-garden-location/

Petersik, J. (2011, August 22). *Making A Compost Bin From Pallets.* Young House Love. https://www.younghouselove.com/a-pallet-able-compost-post/

Piedmont Healthcare. (2021). *The Mind-Body Benefits of Learning A New Skill.* Www.piedmont.org. https://www.piedmont.org/living-better/the-mind-body-benefits-of-learning-a-new-skill

Plant, L. (2021). Ho Farms Pickled Goods. In *Unsplash.* https://unsplash.com/photos/TZw891-oMio

Pleasant, B. (2018, November 10). *Soil pH for Organic Gardeners.*

GrowVeg. https://www.growveg.com/guides/soil-ph-for-organic-gardeners/

Poindexter, J. (2021). *Rabbit Care Guide: 10 Tips to Care for Your Backyard Meat Rabbits*. Morning Chores. https://morningchores.com/meat-rabbit-care/

Raposo, J. (2018, August 10). *Everything You Need to Know About Keeping Bees and Producing Your Own Honey*. Serious Eats. https://www.seriouseats.com/how-to-raise-bees-honey-beekeeping-introduction

Rural Living Today. (2020, September 2). *Best States for Homesteading ~ Know Your Options*. Rural Living Gardening | Hydroponics | Generators. https://rurallivingtoday.com/homesteading-today/best-states-for-homesteading/

Rural Living Today. (2021, July 26). *Free Land ~ How to Find Free Land for Homesteading*. Rural Living Gardening | Hydroponics | Generators. https://rurallivingtoday.com/homesteading-today/free-land/

Sayner, A. (2020, January 18). *Urban Farming Ultimate Guide and Examples*. GroCycle. https://grocycle.com/urban-farming/

Schaeffer, Z. (2021). Greenhouse. In *Unsplash*. https://unsplash.com/photos/siD6uufCyt8

Sessler, J. (2021). Glass Containers Filled with Dry Food. In *Unsplash*. https://unsplash.com/photos/Zjyx5CYVcho

Skye, J. (2021). *Free Chicken Coop Blueprints*. LoveToKnow. https://greenliving.lovetoknow.com/Free_Chicken_Coop_Blueprints

Smith, I. (2020). Raised Garden Beds. In *Unsplash*. https://unsplash.com/photos/JQ7Ng6OgzDM

Spiske, M. (2019). Raised Bed. In *Unsplash*. https://unsplash.com/photos/2XZ-tIRRt04

The Brewers. (2019). Chickens in a chicken coop at our family's farm. In *Unsplash*. https://unsplash.com/photos/kab6rZITjaI

The Cape Coop Farm. (2016, March 30). *Backyard Ducks for Absolute Beginners*. The Cape Coop. https://thecapecoop.com/backyard-ducks-for-absolute-beginners/

The National Center for Home Food Preservation. (n.d.). *Curing *and Smoking Meats for Home Food Preservation.* Nchfp.uga.edu. https://nchfp.uga.edu/publications/nchfp/lit_rev/cure_smoke_pres.html

Thomas, R. B. (2019). *The Old Farmer's Almanac 2020.* Yankee Publishing Inc.

Tyrväinen, L., Ojala, A., Korpela, K., Lanki, T., Tsunetsugu, Y., & Kagawa, T. (2014). The influence of urban green environments on stress relief measures: A field experiment. *Journal of Environmental Psychology, 38,* 1–9. https://doi.org/10.1016/j.jenvp.2013.12.005

U.S. Energy Information Administration. (2021). *Frequently Asked Questions (FAQs) - U.S. Energy Information Administration (EIA).* Www.eia.gov. https://www.eia.gov/tools/faqs/faq.php?id=97&t=3#:~:text=In%202020%2C%20the%20average%20annual

Urban Gardens. (2021, March 3). *How Urban Farms Can Harness the Sun's Energy.* Urban Gardens. https://www.urbangardensweb.com/2021/03/03/how-urban-farms-can-harness-the-suns-energy/

USDA. (2020). *USDA Plant Hardiness Zone Map.* Usda.gov. https://planthardiness.ars.usda.gov/

Winkler, M. (2020). Rural Farm. In *Unsplash.* https://unsplash.com/photos/XDPjmeRj7bQ

Wise, A. (2014, June 22). *Here's Proof Going Outside Makes You Healthier.* HuffPost Canada; HuffPost Canada. https://www.huffpost.com/entry/how-the-outdoors-make-you_n_5508964

Young, M. (2017, January 31). *9 things to learn about backyard meat pigs.* Farm Fit Living. https://farmfitliving.com/things-to-learn-about-backyard-pigs/

REFERENCES

5 benefits of herbal medicine. (2020, May 22). Pinkham Medical. https://pinkhammedical.com/blog/5-benefits-of-herbal-medicine/

5 reasons why we need healthcare professionals now more than ever. (2020, November 4). The George Washington University School of Business. https://healthcaremba.gwu.edu/blog/5-reasons-why-we-need-healthcare-professionals-now-more-than-ever/

10 health issues caused by bad oral health. (2021, October 11). Absolute Dental. https://www.absolutedental.com/blog/10-health-issues-caused-by-bad-oral-health/

12 natural ways to defeat allergies. (2021, February 18). WebMD. https://www.webmd.com/allergies/allergy-education-17/slideshow-natural-relief

50 mind-blowing true survival stories (hiking, kidnapping, lost at sea, plane crashes and more). (2020, June 30). Trek Baron. https://trek-baron.com/survival-stories/

A brief history of medicine. (2013, August 8). FutureLearn. https://www.futurelearn.com/info/courses/study-medicine/0/steps/147884

Altitude sickness. (2020, September 23). Cleveland Clinic. https://my.clevelandclinic.org/health/diseases/15111-altitude-sickness

Andrea, S. (2017). *Snow covered mountain during sunrise.* Pexels. [Image]. https://www.pexels.com/photo/snow-covered-mountain-during-sunrise-618833/

Barbosa, C. (2019). *Close-up photo of woman with her eyes closed holding her forehead.* Pexels. [Image]. https://www.pexels.com/photo/close-up-photo-of-woman-with-her-eyes-closed-holding-her-forehead-2023128/

Basic first aid skills—identifying and addressing altitude sickness. (2016, October 10). Adventure equipped. https://www.adventuremedicalkits.com/blog/2016/10/basic-first-aid-skills-identifying-and-addressing-altitude-sickness/

Bedosky, L. (2021, November 5). *8 ways to keep your immune system healthy.* EverydayHealth. https://www.everydayhealth.com/columns/white-seeber-grogan-the-remedy-chicks/ten-simple-natural-ways-to-boost-immune-system/

Biological hazard. (2021). In *Wikipedia.* https://en.wikipedia.org/wiki/Biological_hazard

Bones, muscles, and joints. (2012, October). Rady Children's Hospital, San Diego. https://www.rchsd.org/health-articles/bones-muscles-and-joints-2/

Bones, muscles and joints. (2021, September). Healthdirect. https://www.healthdirect.gov.au/bones-muscles-and-joints

Brazier, Y. (2020, November 29). *Anatomy: A brief introduction.* MedicalNewsToday. https://www.medicalnewstoday.com/articles/248743

Breathing difficulties—first aid. (2021, November 20). MedlinePlus. https://medlineplus.gov/ency/article/000007.htm

Buer, S. (2016, June 3). *27 considerations for a wilderness first aid kit.* NOLS Blog. https://blog.nols.edu/2016/06/03/27-considerations-for-a-first-aid-kit

Burns, L. (2009, November 5). *First aid in the era of biohazards.* Industrial Safety & Hygiene News. https://www.ishn.com/articles/88912-first-aid-in-the-era-of-biohazards#:~:text=Use%20germicidal%20towelettes%20or%20bleach

Chemical emergency preparedness. (2018). American Red Cross.

https://www.redcross.org/get-help/how-to-prepare-for-emergen-cies/types-of-emergencies/chemical-emergency.html

Chemical hazard. (2021). In *Wikipedia.* https://en.wikipedia.org/wiki/Chemical_hazard

Chronic fatigue syndrome. (2020, September 24). Mayo Clinic. https://www.mayoclinic.org/diseases-conditions/chronic-fatigue-syndrome/symptoms-causes/syc-20360490

Cormier, S. (2017, April 18). *Disaster preparedness: 5 key components to effective emergency management.* HealthcareDive. https://www.healthcaredive.com/news/disaster-preparedness-5-key-components-to-effective-emergency-management/440672/

cottonbro. (2017). *Man putting on coveralls.* Pexels. [Image]. https://www.pexels.com/photo/man-putting-on-coveralls-3951417/

cottonbro. (2020). *Woman in white shirt holding silver pin.* Pexels. [Image]. https://www.pexels.com/photo/fashion-man-people-woman-5721551/

cottonbro. (2021). *Person holding allergy medicine bottle.* Pexels. [Image]. https://www.pexels.com/photo/person-holding-allergy-medicine-bottle-6865181/

Decker, S. (2018, June 5). *Into the woods: Top tips for wilderness medi-cine.* AAFP. https://www.aafp.org/news/blogs/freshperspectives/entry/20180605fp-wilderness.html

Frostbite. (2021, October 9). Mayo Clinic. https://www.mayoclinic.org/diseases-conditions/frostbite/symptoms-causes/syc-20372656

Gómez, O. (2018). *Man on top of mountain.* Pexels. [Image]. https://www.pexels.com/photo/man-on-top-of-mountain-840667/

Grabowska, K. (2020). *Crop unrecognizable male doctor with stetho-scope.* Pexels. [Image]. https://www.pexels.com/photo/crop-unrecognizable-male-doctor-with-stethoscope-4021775/

Grabowska, K. (2021, January 28) *photo-of-a-dentist-demonstrating-how-to-brush-teeth.* Pexels. [Image]. https://www.pexels.com/photo/photo-of-a-dentist-demonstrating-how-to-brush-teeth-6627313/

Herbs to support healthy female hormone balance through all life stage. (2021, September 17). Gaia Herbs. https://www.gaiaherbs.-

com/blogs/seeds-of-knowledge/herbs-to-support-female-hormone-balance-through-all-life-stages

Home remedies for a sprained ankle. (2019, May 17). Top 10 Home Remedies. https://www.top10homeremedies.com/home-remedies/home-remedies-sprained-ankle.html

Home remedies: What works? (2021, February 18). WebMD. https://www.webmd.com/balance/ss/slideshow-home-remedies

How does naturopathic medicine lower health care costs? (n.d.). Institute for Natural Medicine. https://naturemed.org/faq/faq-how-does-naturopathic-medicine-lower-health-care-costs/

Hyponatremia. (2020, May 23). MayoClinic. https://www.mayoclinic.org/diseases-conditions/hyponatremia/symptoms-causes/syc-20373711

Hypothermia. (2020, April 18). Mayo Clinic. https://www.mayoclinic.org/diseases-conditions/hypothermia/diagnosis-treatment/drc-20352688

Immovable joint. (2021, June 28). Biology Online. https://www.biologyonline.com/dictionary/immovable-joint

Insomnia. (2016, October 15). Mayo Clinic. https://www.mayoclinic.org/diseases-conditions/insomnia/symptoms-causes/syc-20355167

Jaspers, E. (2020, April 5). *Adaptability: When change is the only constant.* WeAreBrain. https://wearebrain.com/blog/our-company/adaptability-when-change-is-the-only-constant/

Khongchum, C. (2020). *Photo of female scientist working on laboratory.* Pexels. [Image]. https://www.pexels.com/photo/photo-of-female-scientist-working-on-laboratory-3938023/

Kim, J.H. (2018, July 2). Three principles for radiation safety: Time, distance, and shielding. *The Korean Journal of Pain*, 31(3), 145-146. https://www.ncbi.nlm.nih.gov/pmc/articles/PMC6037814/

Kisan, R., Sujan, M., Adoor, M., Raghavendra, R., Nalini, A., Kutty, B., Chindanda Murthy, B., Raju, TR., & Sathyaprabha, T. (2014). Effect of Yoga on migraine: A comprehensive study using clinical profile and cardiac autonomic functions. *International Journal of Yoga*, 7(2), 126-132. https://doi.org/10.4103/0973-6131.133891

Kuballa, J. (2018, February 4). *18 remedies to get rid of headaches naturally.* Healthline. https://www.healthline.com/nutrition/headache-remedies

Lipman, G. S., Eifling, K. P., Ellis, M. A., Gaudio, F. G., Otten, E. M., & Grissom, C. K. (2014). Wilderness Medical Society practice guidelines for the prevention and treatment of heat-related illness: 2014 Update. *Wilderness & Environmental Medicine*, 25(4), 355–365. https://doi.org/10.1016/j.wem.2014.07.017

Macwelch, T. (2021, April 20). *Survival skills: How to make a mud cast in 4 steps.* OutdoorLife. https://www.outdoorlife.com/blogs/survivalist/survival-skills-how-make-mud-cast-4-steps/

Myers, T., & Hoffman, M. (2015, April 29). Hiker fatality from severe hyponatremia in Grand Canyon National Park. *Wilderness and Environmental Medicine*, 26(3), 371-374. https://www.wemjournal.org/article/S1080-6032(15)00117-9/fulltext

Monstera. (2021). *World map made of tablets and capsules and little lock.* Pexels. [Image]. https://www.pexels.com/photo/world-map-made-of-tablets-and-capsules-and-little-lock-7411935/

Naturopathy. (2021). In *Wikipedia.* https://en.wikipedia.org/wiki/Naturopathy

Naturopathy less expensive than conventional medicine in the long run. (2020, January 9). Express Healthcare. https://www.expresshealthcare.in/interviews/naturopathy-less-expensive-than-conventional-medicine-in-the-long-run/416093/

nhinkle. (2015, December 6). *How to create a cast or splint to aid a broken bone?* [Online forum post]. StackExchange. https://outdoors.stackexchange.com/questions/10145/how-to-create-a-cast-or-splint-to-aid-a-broken-bone

Nierenberg, C. (2016, October 27). *7 strategies for outdoor lovers with seasonal allergies.* Livescience. https://www.livescience.com/56607-outdoor-lovers-seasonal-allergies-tips.html

Ogino, K. (2020). *Tourists talking to each other in forest.* Pexels. [Image]. https://www.pexels.com/photo/tourists-talking-to-each-other-in-forest-5064636/

Ong, C. (2015, January 9). *5 benefits of strategic planning*. Envisio. https://envisio.com/blog/benefits-of-strategic-planning/

Pixabay. (2016, December 21). *Emergency signage*. Pexels. [Image]. https://www.pexels.com/photo/ambulance-architecture-building-business-263402/

Ponsford, S. (2017, December 14). *How to treat a toothache at home*. Medical News Today. https://www.medicalnewstoday.com/articles/320315

Productions, R. (2021a). *Paramedic performing CPR*. Pexels. [Image]. https://www.pexels.com/photo/paramedic-performing-cpr-6520071/

Productions, R. (2021b). *Person applying bandage on another person's hand*. Pexels. [Image]. https://www.pexels.com/photo/person-applying-bandage-on-another-person-s-hand-6519905/

Protecting yourself from radiation. (2021, May 21). EPA. https://www.epa.gov/radiation/protecting-yourself-radiation

RF._.studio (2019, October 10)). *Photo of woman studying anatomy*. Pexels. [Image]. https://www.pexels.com/photo/photo-of-woman-studying-anatomy-3059750/

RF._.studio (2020, February 28). *Unrecognizable African American scientist studying anatomy with tablet*. Pexels. [Image]. https://www.pexels.com/photo/unrecognizable-african-american-scientist-studying-anatomy-with-tablet-3825539/

Ryser, S. (2019, March 7). *Basic first aid skills everyone should learn*. Idaho Medical Academy. https://www.idahomedicalacademy.com/basic-first-aid-skills-everyone-should-learn/

Sarnacki, A. (2019, September 5). *10 medicinal plants for your natural first aid kit*. Hello Homestead. https://hellohomestead.com/10-medicinal-plants-for-your-natural-first-aid-kit/

Schimelpfenig, T. (2020, September 18). *How to treat insect bites and stings*. REI CO OP. https://www.rei.com/learn/expert-advice/how-to-treat-insect-bites-and-stings.html

Shah, N., Hussain, S., Cooke, M., O'Hara, J. P., & Mellor, A. (2015). Wilderness medicine at high altitude: Recent developments in the field. *Open Access Journal of Sports Medicine, 6,* 319–328. https://doi. org/10.2147/OAJSM.S89856

ShemSeger. (2015, December 4). *How to create a cast or splint to aid a broken bone?* [Online forum post]. StackExchange. https://outdoors. stackexchange.com/questions/10145/how-to-create-a-cast-or-splint-to-aid-a-broken-bone

Shuraev, Y. (2021). *Person walking on snow covered field while wearing cold wear.* Pexels. [Image]. https://www.pexels.com/photo/person-walking-on-snow-covered-field-while-wearing-cold-wear-7042404/

Sieroslawska, A. (2021, October 28). *Bones.* Kenhub. https://www.kenhub.com/en/library/anatomy/bones

Stickler, T. (2020, June 4). *Migraine herbal home remedies from around the world.* Healthline. https://www.healthline.com/health/migraine-herbal-home-remedies-from-around-the-world

Tankilevitch, P. (2020). *Person holding thermometer.* Pexels. [Image]. https://www.pexels.com/photo/person-holding-thermometer-3873188/

The Editors of Encyclopedia Britannica. (2020, September 8). *Pulmonary circulation.* Britannica. https://www.britannica.com/science/pulmonary-circulation

The five worst nuclear disasters in history. (2014, July 30). Process Industry Forum. https://www.processindustryforum.com/energy/five-worst-nuclear-disasters-history

The human body. (2020, December 2). Healthline. https://www.healthline.com/human-body-maps#reproductive-system-female

Thomas, A. (2012, April 18). *Medicine and surgery before 1800—the Enlightenment.* homeobook. https://www.homeobook.com/medicine-and-surgery-before-1800-the-enlightenment/

Thompson, W., Underwood, E.A., Richardson, R., Guthrie, D., Rhodes, P., & The Editors of Encyclopedia Britannica. (2020, August 27). *History of Medicine.* Britannica. https://www.britannica.com/science/history-of-medicine/Traditional-medicine-and-surgery-in-Asia

Tips to get rid of a headache. (2015, December 29). WebMD. https://

www.webmd.com/migraines-headaches/5-ways-to-get-rid-of-headache

Tomczak, M. (2004). *Lecture 9: The quest for health, the dawn of medical science.* Incois.gov.in. https://incois.gov.in/Tutor/science+society/lectures/lecture9.html

Torn ligament—causes, symptoms, and treatment. (2010, March 17). HealthHearty. https://healthhearty.com/torn-ligament

Types of bone. (n.d.). Lumen. https://courses.lumenlearning.com/wm-biology2/chapter/types-of-bone/

Types of fractures. (2019, March 28). Complete Care. https://www.visitcompletecare.com/blog/types-of-fractures/

Urinary tract infections. (2010). https://www.kidney.org/sites/default/files/uti.pdf

user5330. (2015, December 6). *How to create a cast or splint to aid a broken bone?* [Online forum post]. StackExchange. https://outdoors.stackexchange.com/questions/10145/how-to-create-a-cast-or-splint-to-aid-a-broken-bone

Vaitkevich, N. (2021). *Flat lay photo of alternative medicines.* Pexels. [Image]. https://www.pexels.com/photo/flat-lay-photo-of-alternative-medicines-7615463/

Van Sloun, N. (2015, November 28). *Natural remedies for everyday illness.* AllinaHealth. https://www.allinahealth.org/healthysetgo/heal/natural-remedies-for-everyday-illnesses

Wachtel-Galor, S. & Benzie, F. (2011). *Chapter 1: Herbal medicine.* NCBI. https://www.ncbi.nlm.nih.gov/books/NBK92773/

Welby, M. (2020, March 17). *The anxious patient: How to calm a patient down to improve care.* Wolters Kluwer. https://www.wolterskluwer.com/en/expert-insights/the-anxious-patient-how-to-calm-a-patient-down-to-improve-care

Welz, A. N., Emberger-Klein, A., & Menrad, K. (2018). Why people use herbal medicine: Insights from a focus-group study in Germany. *BMC Complementary and Alternative Medicine,* 18(92). https://doi.org/10.1186/s12906-018-2160-6

What is a biohazard? Six examples. (2021, April 9). Helix Solutions.

https://www.helixsolutions.net.au/news-and-resources/article/what-is-a-biohazard-six-examples

What is natural medicine? (2021, April 26). Health Times. https://healthtimes.com.au/hub/natural-medicine/72/guidance/ht1/what-is-natural-medicine/2115/

What to do in an emergency. (2020, February 13). NHSinform. https://www.nhsinform.scot/illnesses-and-conditions/heart-and-blood-vessels/heart-emergencies/what-to-do-in-an-emergency

Who should choose a Healthcare MBA? (2017, October 26). The George Washington University School of Business. https://healthcaremba.gwu.edu/

World Health Organization. (2019). *WHO global report on traditional and complementary medicine 2019.* https://www.who.int/traditional-complementary-integrative-medicine/WhoGlobalReportOnTraditionalAndComplementaryMedicine2019.pdf

Worldspectrum. (2018, May 23). *Beige python on brown branch of tree.* Pexels. [Image]. https://www.pexels.com/photo/beige-python-on-brown-branch-of-tree-110819/

Yeast infection in men (balanitis). (2017, June 7). STD. https://www.std-gov.org/stds/yeast_in_man.htm

www.ingramcontent.com/pod-product-compliance
Lightning Source LLC
Chambersburg PA
CBHW060905120626
46553CB00001B/218